U.Urban

READINGS FROM EMILE DURKHEIM

KEY TEXTS

Series Editor: Peter Hamilton
The Open University

KEY TEXTS
Series Editor: PETER HAMILTON
The Open University, Milton Keynes

Designed, like *Key Ideas,* to complement *Key Sociologists,* this series provides concise and original selections from the works of sociologists featured in *Key Sociologists.* The selections, made by the authors of *Key Sociologists* volumes, will enable the books to be used as part of a teaching package connecting study of the essential texts to introductory analyses of the sociologists' works.

READINGS FROM TALCOTT PARSONS
PETER HAMILTON, The Open University, Milton Keynes

READINGS FROM EMILE DURKHEIM
KENNETH THOMPSON, Faculty of Social Science, The Open University, Milton Keynes

READINGS FROM THE FRANKFURT SCHOOL
TOM BOTTOMORE, Professor of Sociology, University of Sussex

READINGS FROM EMILE DURKHEIM

Editor:

KENNETH THOMPSON
Reader in Sociology
The Open University

New translations by
MARGARET A. THOMPSON

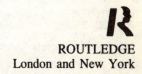

ROUTLEDGE
London and New York

First published in 1985 by Ellis Horwood Ltd
and Tavistock Publications Ltd

Simultaneously published in the USA and Canada
by Routledge
a division of Routledge, Chapman and Hall, Inc.
29 West 35th Street, New York, NY 10001

Reprinted 1989, and 1991 by Routledge

Typeset by Ellis Horwood Ltd
Printed in Great Britain by Richard Clay Ltd, Bungay, Suffolk

British Library Cataloguing in Publication Data

Durkheim, Emile
Readings from Emile Durkheim. – (Key texts)
1. Sociology
I. Title II. Thompson, Kenneth, 1937–
III. Series
301 HM51

Library of Congress Card No. 85–8429

ISBN 0-415-04320-4

Contents

KENNETH THOMPSON is Reader in Sociology at the Open University, Milton Keynes. He graduated from the University of Leicester in 1963 with a B.A. in Social Sciences, and was awarded a D. Phil. in Sociology in 1967 by the University of Oxford.

He was Assistant Professor of Rutgers University, New Jersey, USA, from 1967 to 1968, and at Smith College, Massachusetts, USA, from 1968 to 1970. He took up his present position in 1970, returning to Smith College as a Visiting Professor for the year 1980–81. He was author, in 1982, of *Emile Durkheim* (Ellis Horwood/Tavistock).

His other publications include works on the subjects of:
Bureaucracy and Church Reform (1970), *Auguste Comte: The Foundation of Sociology* (1976), *Sociological Perspectives* (1971), *People and Organisations* (1973), *Control and Ideology in Organizations* (1980), *An Introduction to Sociology* (1980), *Work, Employment and Unemployment* (1984), and *Sartre: Life and Works* (with M. Thompson, 1984).

Series Editor's Foreword

The series of KEY TEXTS volumes is designed to both introduce the student to the most important work of the Key Sociologists, and to provide representative selections of their writings for all readers. Because the selection of readings contained in KEY TEXTS volumes complements the treatment of the *Key Sociologists* volumes, the two together provide indispensable aids to study and research.

Kenneth Thompson's *Readings from Emile Durkheim* is a comprehensive complement to his earlier and much acclaimed *Emile Durkheim* (Ellis Horwood/Tavistock, 1982) in the *Key Sociologists* series. But it is no mere compilation of material which could be gained from a number of other sources. For Dr Thompson, ably assisted by Margaret Thompson, has prepared new translations of the selections from the central elements of Durkheim's *oeuvre: The Division of Labour in Society* (1893), *The Rules of Sociological Method* (1895), and *Suicide* (1897). Although widely used, the existing translations have long been recognized to be problematic transcriptions of Durkheim's ideas into English, which reveal more perhaps about the intellectual climate for which they were prepared than they do in exposing the full flavour and range of his thinking. In some cases, newer translations of fragments of the work have been published, but it is a distinct asset to the present work that it contains such an extensive selection of material specifically translated for this volume. The Thompsons have published a number of important translations of French sociology (not least from those highly influenced by the Durkheimian school, but also from Durkheim's important predecessor, Auguste Comte). Their work has played an important part in making available to the English-speaking reader a more complete and faithful picture of crucial elements in the development of French sociological thought. This volume thus represents a further stage in that process of the communication and accurate transposition of ideas, theories and concepts from one cultural tradition to another.

Why read Durkheim (or any other sociologist, for that matter) in the original, rather than relying on secondary analyses? The question may seem to be rather more easy to answer than it in fact proves to be, when unpacked a little. The conventional response has always been that it is intellectually valuable to know how the ideas were in fact presented, in order that they might be better understood. It has been traditional to claim that reading *Suicide,* for example, has inspirational value, in helping the student bond more closely with the sociology discipline he or she studies. An alternative view abounded — and is still not uncommon — that the reading of the sociological 'classics' is an indispensable part of the intellectual socialization of anyone interested in the discipline. Finally, and perhaps least valuably, there was the convention that reading fragments of the classics constituted a sort of selective exampling of certain key ideas in the sociological canon. The fact that this might imply reading the material out of context was thought to be of little importance — the crucial thing was to be 'exposed' to the material, and therefore to have allowed the intellectual 'osmosis' from sociological classic to reader to have had an opportunity to take place.

In the selections and translations provided by the Thompsons, the emphasis has been very much on showing a Durkheim whose ideas are challenging to modern conceptions of the discipline. Generations of 'glosses' on Durkheim's work have obscured the fundamental radicalism of much of his sociological thought. This was perhaps meritable, since the ramifications of extensive influence on a developing intellectual discipline are — uninspiringly — a distortion and homogenization of the original insights. As ideas, concepts, theories and models are incorporated into intellectual discourse their meaning changes — especially when they are progressively separated from their contextual framework. Of course, Durkheim has suffered no worse a fate than Marx or Weber — although his work has been tainted somewhat in contemporary terms by its association with functionalism, through which his work has often appeared to be over concerned with order, stability, and solidarity. The radical stance of sociological realism which Durkheim put forward in his classic injunction to 'treat social facts as things' in *The Rules of Sociological Method,* is also diminished by its association with positivism — something which in today's terms seems almost as reactionary as functionalism. But the fact that Durkheim's ideas proved serviceable to earlier (and in their time quite persuasive) paradigms of social thought should not blind the contemporary sociologist to the value of Durkheim's contribution to the development of sociological thought. Nor should it be forgotten that Durkheim's intellectual heritage is very much alive and kicking in the historical studies conceptions of the *Annalistes.* When we pick up a study by Fernand Braudel, Georges Duby or even Emmanuel Le Roy Ladurie, we are close to the spirit of Durkheim's methodological imperatives. The great convergence of history and sociology in the post-war era has been deeply influenced by Durkheimian sentiments.

The contents of this volume constitute a representative and authoratively edited collection of Durkheim's key works. The clarity and readability of the newly translated pieces will be of considerable value to the reader who is new to Durkheim, and to the reader who is aware of the major pieces, but wishes to read them in a translation which is at one and the same time faithful to their original meaning, and sensitive to Durkheim's relevance for contemporary social thought.

Preface

The aim of this book is to present the core of Durkheim's sociology by making available a selection of lengthy key passages from most of his major works. In order to accomplish this it has been necessary to undertake new translations of the passages from three of those works: *De la Division du travail social* (1893), *Les Règles de la méthode sociologique* (1895), and *Le Suicide* (1897). It has long been recognized that the early translations of these works were seriously defective and sometimes misleading. Although new translations have recently begun to appear, or have been announced, it seemed sensible to continue the task we had embarked on of producing an internally consistent set of translations tailored to our own needs and satisfaction rather than risk having to make compromises. Throughout, we have sought to maintain a balance — modernizing Durkheim's language sufficiently to remove obstacles to understanding his meaning, whilst trying to remain faithful to his style of argument and expression. One of the typical results of this policy is that the somewhat ambiguous French term, *conscience collective,* which can refer to both conscience and consciousness, we have translated as 'collective consciousness' in most cases.

Although the translations have required close collaboration, Margaret Thompson deserves most of the credit. This is the fourth book on which we have collaborated to produce translations of French sociology and I would like to pay tribute to her skills as a translator and scholar — qualities which she is too modest to lay claim to on her own behalf.

Finally, I would like to acknowledge the intellectual debt I owe to Anthony Giddens, one which now stretches back over two decades to the period when I had the good fortune to be one of his first students in the flourishing Sociology Department at the University of Leicester.

Kenneth Thompson
3 March, 1985

For Clare

Introduction

In the short space of about 25 years, from the last decade of the nineteenth century through to the 1914–18 War, it is arguable that Emile Durkheim contributed more to the founding of modern sociology than any other individual before or since. He defined and demonstrated its method in a series of brilliant studies, most notably: *The Division of Labour in Society* (1893), *The Rules of Sociological Method* (1895), *Suicide* (1897), and *The Elementary Forms of the Religious Life* (1912). During much of this time he was directing the academic development of sociology throughout France from his influential position at the University of Paris, to which he had moved from Bordeaux in 1902. His influence was consolidated through the journal that he founded in 1898, *L'Année sociologique,* which was read not only by sociologists in France, but also by scholars in other disciplines and other countries.

Although this influence as a founding father of the academic discipline of sociology is generally acknowledged, it has not always been welcomed. Unlike the man himself, who was admired for his seriousness and integrity as 'the professional conscience personified', his sociology has frequently excited strong reaction and controversy. This is not surprising, as his arguments for a distinctive set of 'facts' that should constitute the subject-matter of sociology, and his description of the appropriate method for studying those facts, were calculated to shock. His views were shocking in two respects: firstly, because his approach was deliberately counter-intuitive and opposed to taken-for-granted assumptions about the nature and causes of social phenomena; secondly, because he was mounting a radical critique of existing schools of thought that had been drawn on as a source of sociological explanation — biology, psychology, economics and utilitarianism. All of these, he argued, were in various ways deficient and misleading guides to sociological understanding. Sociology had to have its own subject-matter or set of fundamental facts to explain, and this could not be 'reduced' to some other discipline's level of facts, such as the biological organism, individual psychology, the economic substratum of material existence (or, alternatively, the purely abstract model of economic man), or to utilitarian philosophy's conception of society as an aggregate of individuals acting rationally in terms of utility and self-interest. It needs to be realized that these were some of the ruling ideas of the period and that Durkheim, in marking out the ground and laying the foundation for modern sociology, had to overcome much resistance from entrenched orthodoxies. In mounting his assault he ran the risk of overstating his case, and some of the criticisms both then and since can be understood as reactions to this tendency. This applies particularly to his injunction that social facts should be regarded as 'things', and that these facts are the emergent properties of social wholes, which exercise an almost irresistible determining influence on the behaviour of individuals.

The criticisms of this position have come from opposite ends of the spectrum. On the one hand there are those who accuse him of taking up a rationalist—idealist position in which social reality is found at the level of group thought or a collective mind. Located at the other extreme are those of his contemporaries who were so shocked by his seemingly 'materialist' explanation of concepts and beliefs as being shaped by factors such as the distribution and density of population, the organization of social relationships, and the experience of social interaction, that they regarded his position as little different from the 'materialism' of Karl Marx. In early American sociology he was criticized for his supposedly excessive social realism, which went against the prevailing individulistic and voluntaristic tradition. Until his work was rendered into a more palatable, and less radical, form by Talcott Parsons and other commentators, he was regarded as suspiciously radical. To European sociologists, who began to revive Marxist and neo-Marxist social theory after the Second World War, his sociology seemed too preoccupied with the functionalist concern for social solidarity and the conservation of society, and so inherently conservative. Where does the truth lie? A balanced answer can only be arrived at after studying key passages from all his major works (such as those provided in this volume). However, it is certainly not the case that Durkheim's approach proved to be unrewarding and restrictive for sociology. On the contrary, the proof of its fecundity is to be found in the rich and varied studies that it stimulated in so many areas of sociological research. The richness of Durkheim's legacy to sociology can only be grasped after a 'positive' or sympathetic reading of the key works. Appreciation must come before criticism. (Some of the main criticisms of Durkheim's sociology are discussed in the companion volume (Thompson, 1982) [1].) The following comments can be regarded as an introduction or guide to such a reading.

THE NATURE OF DURKHEIM'S SOCIOLOGY

Although Durkheim wrote a great deal about how things should be studied in sociology, he never offered a comprehensive definition of the subject commensurate with his model and practice of that discipline. The nearest he came to this was in two brief definitions that appear in *The Rules of Sociological Method*, where he agreed with the formulation of two of his disciples, Mauss and Fouconnet, that,

> Sociology can then be defined as the science of institutions,
> of their genesis and of their functioning. [2]

By 'institutions' he meant 'all beliefs and all modes of conduct instituted by the collectivity' [2].

Sociology could also be defined as the study of social facts, which in turn were defined as follows:

> A social fact is every way of acting, whether fixed or not,
> which is capable of exercising an external constraint on the
> individual; or, which is general throughout a given society,
> whilst having an existence of its own, independent of its individual manifestations. [2]

This definition of sociology as the study of social facts may seem self-evident today, but that may be due to the fact that we have come to accept the point that Durkheim was seeking to establish, which is that there are constraining and determining factors of a social nature that must be taken into account in explaining human behaviour. Durkheim was arguing gainst the prevailing tendency to reduce such explanations to the levels of individual psychology or biology, and the indi-

vidual and voluntaristic philosophies of his time. Hence his emphasis
on *social* facts. Furthermore, by insisting that social *facts* were to be
considered as things, he sought to persuade sociologists to adopt the
detached stance of the scientist, setting aside all preconceptions and
searching for empirical indicators of theoretically conceptualized factors
operating beneath the surface of events. The task of the sociologist
was to disclose and analyse these underlying structures, or structured
tendencies, that determined phenomena and events such as crime and
punishment, suicides, religious beliefs and rituals, etc. Its task, as defined
by Durkheim, therefore, was one of structural analysis. In this respect
his approach resembled that of Karl Marx, as Durkheim himself noted
in his review of a collection of essays by the Italian Marxist, Antonio
Labriola (cf. Reading 2). For example, Durkheim's structural analysis
in *The Division of Labour in Society* traced a fundamental process of
social development which involved the crystallization of patterns of
social relations under pressure from the environment, and the suc-
ceeding crystallization of moral and cognitive categories and norms
from these patterned social relationships. Thus the causal flow was
from material substratum (for example, population density and density
of interaction) via group structure (for example, increased division of
labour) to beliefs and norms (for example, the cult of the individual
and contract law). However, he also stressed that the causal flow could
be in the opposite direction and indeed often was: once symbolic
representations, such as religious beliefs, had come into existence, they
became the causes of other phenomena, the more so as they became
crystallized or institutionalized. From our present vantage point of
greater familiarity with the full range of Marx's writings, and the
many commentaries on them, there is reason to believe Marx would
not have disagreed on that point. Nevertheless, Durkheim was con-
vinced that where he differed from Marx, and from some other early
sociologists, such as Auguste Comte and Herbert Spencer, was in his
caution about offering global theories which elevated one factor to the
level of the 'mainspring of history' or the 'key to history', as he put it.
He believed that predecessors like Comte and Spencer had aroused a
great deal of scepticism towards sociology from other disciplines
because of their 'philosophical meditation on human sociology in
general'. What was needed was more specialization and rigour within
sociology. He stated his intention to draw into sociology's orbit specialists in specific areas of study, such as history and law, who would gain
from adopting a sociological perspective, and, more importantly, who
would supply the data which would enable sociology to practise its own
'experimental' method of mental comparison. By comparing institu-

tions, beliefs, and practices, in different societies, sociology would be able to test hypotheses about their causes and functions. He divided the field of sociology into three principal divisions: social morphology, social physiology, and general sociology. Social morphology was to be concerned with the distribution and organization of people and resources in society — the material substratum. Social physiology subdivided into specialisms concerned with different social institutions — religion, law, economics, etc. General sociology would build on these specific findings and eventually reveal the most general tendencies and laws of social life.

Implicit in Durkheim's discussions of the subject-matter of sociology and of the subdivisions of its study was a model of the continuum of social phenomena ranged in levels downwards from the surface level of the most crystallized down to the more obscure levels of the least crystallized social phenomena. This multi-layered model of social phenomena or social facts can be expressed as follows:

I. *Morphology (substratum)*
Volume, density and distribution of population. Territorial organization. Material objects incorporated in the society: buildings, channels of communication, monuments, technological instruments (e.g. machines, etc.).

II. *Institutions (normative sphere)*
(a) Formal rules and norms — expressed in fixed legal and sub-legal formulae, moral precepts, religious dogmas, political and economic forms, professional role definitions — or in determining language conventions and obligations of social categories.
(b) Informal rules and norms as applied in the preceding domains: customary models, collective habits and beliefs.

III. *Collective representations (symbolic sphere)*
(a) Societal values, collective ideals; opinions; representations which the society has of itself; legends and myths; religious representations (symbols, etc.).
(b) Free currents of social life that are effervescent and not yet caught in a definite mould; creative collective thinking; values and representations in the process of emerging.

(this model is discussed more fully in Thompson (1982) [1].)

This is a schematic outline of the subject-matter of sociology or of the range of social facts. The basic characteristics of social facts, as spelt out in *The Rules of Sociological Method,* are: externality, constraint, and generality. They have an existence external to any individual or the mind of any individual. They exercise constraint over the individual in various ways, depending on their position within the continuum of social phenomena ranging from morphological facts that determine the availability of resources, to the constraining force of norms backed by sanctions, to the constraints imposed by language, the force of myths and symbols, and the pressure of public opinion. There are basically two modes of constraint: the constraint imposed by lack of choice, and the pressure to choose according to established notions of what ought to be the case. Morphological factors exercise the first sort of constraint, usually through the form and distribution of material resources. Institutions and collective representations, such as normative routines, beliefs, and currents of opinion, exercise the other type of constraint. However, some social facts exercise both kinds of constraint, a combination of material resource limitation and moral pressure to act in a certain way; an example would be the provision by a college of only single-sex accommodation for students.

In his first two major works, the *Division of Labour* and the *Rules*, he inclined towards a 'generic' materialism, an explanatory framework in which the more concrete and 'objective' elements are seen as causes of those which are more abstract and conceptual. However, even at this early stage in his development of an explanatory method, he made clear that whilst morphological factors may have been preponderant in originating an institution, they did not continue to determine its present shape and functioning. He increasingly developed his conception of collective representations (ideas, norms, values, and beliefs, etc.) as a crucial and relatively independent set of explanatory variables, thus refining his original broad notion of the collective *conscience* (this French word means both 'consciousness' and 'conscience'). This was facilitated, after he had written the *Rules*, as he acquired more comparative data, particularly ethnographic data on the potency and variety of collective representations of a religious nature in primitive societies. He also broadened the sense of morphology to include underlying structures that were a fusion of material and mental factors. So that, between the various levels of social phenomena, from the morphological substructure to the most fluid currents of social life, there were only differences in degree of consolidation or crystallization.

Each of his major works was intended to demonstrate the sociological method for disclosing relationships between the different layers of the total social phenomenon. In the *Division of Labour* it is relationships between such factors as population density (including density of interactions), specialization of functions, and the legal and penal institutions. In the *Rules* he discusses the method in more detail and gives illustrations relating to the division of labour and suicide. *Suicide* itself is used to demonstrate that complex structural relationships, including those between fluid suicidogenic currents and institutions such as religion and the family, can be plotted by using the empirical indicator of differential suicide rates. The underlying theme, as in the other works, is the way in which structural forces affect the level of social integration (relationships between individuals and society). Low suicide rates reveal a 'healthy' level of integration, evidence that the relationships are in a state of equilibrium, exerting neither too strong nor too weak a force on the individual; high suicide rates reveal a pathological state of disequilibrium. In his last great work, *The Elementary Forms of the Religious Life,* he uses his structuralist method to trace relationships between morphological facts, social organization, religious beliefs and other collective representations (including concepts of space, time, and causation). Apart from their effective demonstration of the Durkheimian sociological method, these studies are full of thought-provoking and counter-intuitive findings. In the *Division of Labour* it is suggested that punishment of crime is designed to act more on the law-abiding citizen than on the criminal. Among the findings in *Suicide* is one which suggests that marriage is harmful to women (without children) judging by the suicide rate; economic booms increase suicides, whereas revolutions and wars do not. *The Elementary Forms of the Religious Life* uses evidence on totemism among Australian aborigines and American indians to explore the social functions of religion, but also produces a sociology of knowledge which not only suggests that our ideas of God are collective representations of the social order itself, but so are our ideas of time, space, and causation.

Similar challenging findings are presented in his works dealing with other social institutions, such as political and economic organization in *Professional Ethics and Civic Morals* and *Socialism,* and on education in *The Evolution of Educational Thought* and *Moral Education.* In the case of political and economic issues, Durkheim adopts a much more radical approach than he is often given credit for; he should not be identified with an approach preoccupied with 'order' and 'stability', for the purpose of making an oversimplified contrast with Marx, who is then portrayed as concerned with 'conflict' and 'change'. The analysis developed in *Professional Ethics and Civic Morals* is a direct continuation of that begun in the *Division of Labour.* Far from wishing to defend 'order' against change, or being sanguine about the present social order, his critical sociological analysis had the objective of helping society to see what had to be done to achieve change and to escape from a pathological condition. The differentiation of institutions and functions entailed in the modernizing process of the division of labour had produced a situation marked by greatly increased individualism. This could be a positive development or it could have pathological results, depending on the type of individualism that prevailed. As it had developed in France and other capitalist societies it had taken on pathological characteristics − egoism rather than moral individualism threatened to predominate. It was each man for himself, rather than each for every other. Competition and conflict to satisfy individual, unrestrained appetites and ambitions reigned in place of cooperation to promote the common good. Freedom of contract in this situation of inequality simply meant that the strong exploited the weak. The ideals of moral individualism could only be fulfilled if society was organized and people educated in such a way as to enable the individuals to govern themselves, that is to control the appetites and be free to realize their potential and to assist others to do the same. This is also the theme in his analysis in *Socialism,* and in his writings on education.

Although Durkheim's writings on politics and education are important for gaining a balanced view of his position, they do not have the same stature as his major works, partly because of the fact that they were not finished works but posthumous publications based on lecture notes. It is also the case that the three major works dealing with substantive topics − *Division of Labour, Suicide* and *Elementary Forms* − all have a similar structure of argument, despite the differences in topic and data. It can be briefly outlined as follows. In each work the argument is arranged in three parts. First, he gives a definition of the subject-matter. Secondly, he presents various suggested explanations of the phenomenon, usually of a psychologistic or individualistic explanatory nature. He then uses a combination of argument and data to show the inadequacy of these explanations, as, for example, with the thesis that the division of labour results from the pursuit of increased happiness, that suicide rates are explicable in terms of insanity, and that religion can be seen as the outgrowth of natural or cosmic forces. Finally, in each case he puts forward his own sociological explanation in which the social fact in question − the growth in the division of labour, the different rates of suicide, totemic beliefs and practices − are explained in terms of other social facts. In the *Division of Labour* the growth in population volume, population density, and then in 'moral density', produces a growth in social differentiation, specialization of functions, and the emergence of organic solidarity based on complementarity of the parts, in contrast to the mechanical solidarity of more primitive societies, which was based on resemblance of the parts and the dominance of the collective consciousness over individuals. This also explains the change in the character of law and punishment, from the repressive type under mechanical solidarity to the restitutive type characteristic of societies bound by organic solidarity. In *Suicide* the comparative rates of suicide, as between such groups as Catholics and Protestants, married and unmarried people, rich and poor, and as between periods of national crisis or relative quiet, are determined by different suicidogenic currents related to four types of imbalance in the relation of the individual to society: one pair relates to the degree of integration or interaction in a group (egoism – too little; and altruism – too much), the other pair refers to the degree of moral regulation (anomie – too little; and fatalism – too much); while in the *Elementary Forms* he argues that religion serves certain functional needs that bind people together, and that what people worship is really society itself.

Occasionally, some of Durkheim's arguments and his mode of expressing them can tend to seem rather quaint today, but the key passages of his main works still have a capacity to challenge and instruct any reader with a genuine interest in sociology's contribution to understanding the world in which we live.

REFERENCES

[1] Kenneth Thompson (1982) *Emile Durkheim,* London, Tavistock/Ellis Horwood; New York, Methuen.
[2] Cf. extract from Emile Durkheim, *The Rules of Sociological Method,* Reading 5 in this volume.

Part One

Sociology - its nature and programme

Reading 1

SOCIOLOGY AND THE SOCIAL SCIENCES

Now on first consideration, sociology might appear indistinguishable from psychology; and this thesis has in fact been maintained, by Tarde, among others. Society, they say, is nothing but the individuals of whom it is composed. They are its only reality. How, then, can the science of societies be distinguished from the science of individuals, that is to say, from psychology?

If one reasons in this way, one could equally well maintain that biology is but a chapter of physics and chemistry, for the living cell is composed exclusively of atoms of carbon, nitrogen, and so on, which the physico-chemical sciences undertake a study. But that is to forget that a whole very often has very different properties from those which its constituent parts possess. Though a cell contains nothing but mineral elements, these reveal, by being combined in a certain way, properties which they do not have when they are not thus combined and which are characteristic of life (properties of sustenance and of reproduction); they thus form, through their synthesis, a reality

Edited and reprinted with permission from: M. Traugott (ed.), *Emile Durkheim On Institutional Analysis,* Chicago, University of Chicago Press, 1977, pp. 76–83. Originally published as 'Sociologie et sciences sociales', in *De la Méthode dans les sciences,* Paris, Alcan, 1909, pp. 259–285.

of an entirely new sort, which is living reality and which constitutes the subject matter of biology. In the same way, individual consciousnesses, by associating themselves in a stable way, reveal, through their interrelationships, a new life very different from that which would have developed had they remained uncombined; this is social life. Religious institutions and beliefs, political, legal, moral, and economic institutions – in a word, all of what constitutes civilization – would not exist if there were no society.

In effect, civilization presupposes cooperation not only among all the members of a single society, but also among all the societies which interact with one another. Moreover, it is possible only if the results obtained by one generation are transmitted to the following generation in such a way that they can be added to the results which the latter will obtain. But for that to happen, the successive generations must not be separated from one another as they arrive at adulthood but must remain in close contact, that is to say, they must be associated in a permanent fashion. Thus, this entire, vast assembly of things exists only because there are human associations; moreover, they vary according to what these associations are, and how they are organized. These things find their immediate explanation in the nature of societies, not of individuals, and constitute, therefore, the subject matter of a new science distinct from, though related to, individual psychology: this is sociology.

Comte was not content to establish these two principles theoretically; he undertook to put them into practice, and, for the first time, he attempted to create a sociological discipline. It is for this purpose that he uses the three final volumes of the *Cours de philosophie positive.* Little remains today of the details of his work. Historical and especially ethnographic knowledge was still too rudimentary in his time to offer a sufficiently solid basis for sociological inductions. Moreover, as we shall see below, Comte did not recognize the multiplicity of the problems posed by the new science: he thought that he could create it all at once, as one would create a system of metaphysics; sociology, however, like any science, can be constituted only progressively, by approaching questions one after another. But the idea was infinitely fertile and outlived the founder of positivism.

It was taken up again first by Herbert Spencer. Then, in the last thirty years, a whole legion of workers arose – to some extent in all countries, but particularly in France – and applied themselves to these studies. Sociology has now left behind the heroic age. The principles on which it rests and which were originally proclaimed in a very philosophical and dialectical way have now received factual confirmation. It assumes that social phenomena are in no way contingent or arbitrary. Sociologists have shown that certain moral and legal institutions and certain religious beliefs are identical everywhere that conditions of social life are identical. They have even been able to establish similarities in the details of the customs of countries very distant from each other and between which there has never been any sort of communication. This remarkable uniformity is the best proof that the social realm does not escape the law of universal determinism.

II. THE DIVISIONS OF SOCIOLOGY: THE INDIVIDUAL SOCIAL SCIENCES

But if, in a sense, sociology is a unified science, still it includes a multiplicity of questions and, consequently, a multiplicity of individual sciences. Therefore, let us examine these sciences of which sociology is the corpus.

Comte already felt the need to divide it up; he distinguished two parts: social statics and social dynamics. Statics studies societies by considering them as fixed at a given point in their development; it seeks the laws of their equilibrium. At each moment in time, the individuals and the groups which shape them are joined to one another by bonds of a certain type, which assure social cohesion; and the various estates of a single civilization maintain definite relations with one another. To a given degree of elaboration of science, for example, corresponds a specific development of religion, morality, art, industry, and so forth. Statics tries to determine what these bonds of solidarity and these connections are. Dynamics, on the contrary, considers societies in their evolution and attempts to discover the law of their development. But the object of statics as Comte understood it is very indeterminate, since it arises from the definition which we have just given; moreover, he devotes only a few pages to it in the *Cours de philosophie*. Dynamics take up all the rest. Now the problem with which dynamics deals is unique: according to Comte, a single and invariable law dominates the course of evolution; this is the famous Law of Three Stages. The sole object of social dynamics is to investigate this law. Thus understood, sociology is reduced to a single question; so much so that once this single question has been resolved — and Comte believed he had found the definitive solution — the science will be complete. Now it is in the very nature of the positive sciences that they are never complete. The realities with which they deal are far too complex ever to be exhausted. If sociology is a positive science, we can be assured that it does not consist in a single problem but includes, on the contrary, different parts, many distinct sciences which correspond to the various aspects of social life.

There are, in reality, as many branches of sociology, as many individual social sciences, as there are different types of social facts. A methodical classification of social facts would be premature and, in any case, will not be attempted here. But it is possible to indicate its principal categories.

First of all, there is reason to study society in its external aspect. From this angle, it appears to be formed by a mass of population of a certain density, disposed in the face of the earth in a certain fashion, dispersed in the countryside or concentrated in cities, and so on. It occupies a more or less extensive territory, situated in a certain way relative to the seas and to the territories of neighbouring peoples, more or less furrowed with waterways and paths of communications of all sorts which place the inhabitants in more or less intimate relationship. This territory, its dimensions, its configuration, and the composition of the population which moves upon its surface are naturally important factors of social life; they are its *substratum* and, just as psychic life in the individual varies with the anatomical composition of the brain which supports it, collective phenomena vary with the constitution of the social substratum. There is, therefore, room for a social science which traces its anatomy; and since this science has as its object the external and material form of society, we propose to call it *social morphology*. Social morphology does not, moreover, have to limit itself to a descriptive analysis; it must also explain. It must look for the reasons why the population is massed at certain points rather than at others, why it is principally urban or principally rural, what are the causes which favor or impede the development of great cities, and so on. We can see that this special science itself has a multitude of problems with which to deal.

But parallel to the substratum of collective life, there is this life itself. Here we run across a distinction analogous to that which we observe in the other natural sciences. Alongside chemistry, which studies the way in which minerals are constituted, there is physics, the subject matter of which is the phenomena of all sorts for which the bodies thus constituted are the theater. In biology, while anatomy (also called morphology) analyzes the structure of living beings and the mode of composition of their tissues and organs, physiology studies the functions of these tissues and organs. In the same way, beside social morphology there is room for a social physiology which studies the vital manifestations of societies.

But social physiology is itself very complex and includes a multiplicity of individual sciences; for the social phenomena of the physiological order are themselves extremely varied.

First there are religious beliefs, practices, and institutions. Religion is, in effect, a social phenomenon, since it has always been a property of a group, namely, a church, and because in the great majority of cases the church and the political society are indistinct. Until very recent times, one was faithful to certain divinities by the very fact that one was the citizen of a certain state. In any case, dogmas and myths have always consisted in systems of beliefs common to an entire collectivity and obligatory for the members of that collectivity. It is the same way with rituals. The study of religion is, therefore, the domain of sociology; it constitutes the subject matter of the *sociology of religion*.

Moral ideas and mores form another category, distinct from the preceding. We shall see in another chapter how the rules of morality are social phenomena; they are the subject matter of the *sociology of morality*.

There is no need to demonstrate the social character of legal institutions. They are to be studied by the *sociology of law*. This field is, moreover, closely related to the sociology of morality, for moral ideas are the spirit of the law. What constitutes the authority of a legal code is the moral idea which it incarnates and which it translates into definite formulations.

Finally, there are the economic institutions: institutions relating to the production of wealth (serfdom, tenant farming, corporate organization, production in factories, in mills, at home, and so on), institutions relating to exchange (commercial organization, markets, stock exchanges, and so on), institutions relating to distribution (rent, interest, salaries, and so on). They form the subject matter of *economic sociology*.

These are the principal branches of sociology. They are not, however, the only ones. Language, which in certain respects depends on organic conditions, is nevertheless a social phenomenon, for it is also the product of a group and it bears its stamp. Even language is, in general, one of the characteristic elements of the physiognomy of societies, and it is not without reason that the relatedness of languages is often used as a means of establishing the relatedness of peoples. There is, therefore, subject matter for a sociological study of language, which has, moreover, already begun. We can say as much of aesthetics, for, despite the fact that each artist (poet, orator, sculptor, painter, and so on) puts his own mark on the works that he creates, all those that are elaborated in the same social milieu and in the same period express in different forms a single ideal which is itself closely related to the temperament of the social groups to which they address themselves.

It is true that certain of these facts are already studied by disciplines long since established; notably, economic facts serve as the subject matter for the assembly of diverse research, analyses, and theories which together are designated as political economy. But just as we said above, political economy has remained to the present a hybrid study, intermediate between art and science; it is much less concerned with observing industrial and commercial life such as it is and has been in order to know it and determines its laws than with reconstructing this life as it should be. The economists have as yet only a quite weak sense that economic reality is imposed upon the observer like physical realities, that it is subject to the same necessity, and that, consequently, the science which studies it must be created in a quite speculative way before we undertake to reform it. What is more, they study facts, which are dealt with as if they formed an independent whole which is self-sufficient and self-explanatory. In reality, economic functions are social functions and are integrated with the other collective functions; they become inexplicable when they are violently removed from that context. Workers' wages depend not only on the relationships of supply and demand but upon certain moral conceptions. They rise or fall depending on the idea we create for ourselves of the individual. More examples could be cited. By becoming a branch of sociology, economic science will naturally be wrenched from its isolation at the same time that it will become more deeply impregnated with the idea of scientific determinism. As a consequence of thus taking its place in the system of the social sciences, it will not merely undergo a change of name; both the spirit which animates it and the methods which it practices will be transformed.

We see from this analysis how false is the view that sociology is but a very simple science which consists, as Comte thought, in a single problem. As of today, it is impossible for a sociologist to possess encyclopaedic knowledge of his science; but each scholar must attach himself to a special order of problems unless he wishes to be content with very general and vague views. These general views may have been useful when sociology was merely trying to explore the limits of its domain and to become aware of itself, but the discipline can no longer dally in such a fashion. This is not to say, however, that there is no place for a synthetic science which will manage to assemble the general conclusion which all these other specific sciences will reveal. As different as the various classes of social facts may be, they are, nonetheless, only species of the same genus; there is, therefore, reason to seek out what makes for the unity of the genus, what characterizes the social fact *in abstracto,* and whether there are very general laws of which the very diverse laws established by the special sciences are only particular forms. This is the object of general sociology, just as general biology has as its object to reveal the most general properties and laws of life. This is the philosophical part of the science. But since the worth of the synthesis depends on the worth of the analyses from which it results, the most urgent task of sociology is to advance this work of analysis.

In summary, table 1 represents in a schematic way the principal divisions of sociology.

Table 1 — Principal divisions of sociology

SOCIAL MORPHOLOGY	The study of the geographic base of various peoples in terms of its relationships with their social organization. The study of population: its volume, its density, and its disposition on the earth.
SOCIAL PHYSIOLOGY	Sociology of Religion Sociology of Morality Sociology of Law Economic Sociology Linguistic Sociology Aesthetic Sociology

GENERAL SOCIOLOGY

[. . .]

The principal problems of sociology consist in researching the way in which a political, legal, moral, economic, or religious institution, belief, and so on, was established, what causes gave rise to it, and to what useful ends it responds.

Reading 2

REVIEW OF ANTONIO LABRIOLA, *ESSAYS ON THE MATERIALIST CONCEPTION OF HISTORY*

We think it a fertile idea that social life must be explained, not by the conception of it created by those who participate in it, but by profound causes which escape awareness; and we also think that these causes must principally be sought in the way in which associated individuals are grouped. It even seems to us that it is on this condition, and on this condition only, that history can become a science and that sociology can, consequently, exist. For, in order that collective representations be intelligible, they must arise from something and, since they cannot form a circle closed upon itself, the source from which they arise must be found outside themselves. Either the collective consciousness floats in a vacuum, a sort of unrepresentable absolute, or it is related to the rest of the world through the intermediary of a substratum on which it consequently depends. From another point of view, of what can this substratum be composed if not of the members of society as they are socially combined? We believe this proposition is self-evident. However, we see no reason to associate it, as the author

From: *Emile Durkheim on Institutional Analysis,* Edited and translated by Mark Traugott, Chicago, University of Chicago Press, 1978, pp. 127–130. Original publication in French as review of A. Labriola, *Essais sur la conception matérialiste de l'histoire, Revue philosophique,* **44** (1897), pp. 645–65.

does, with the socialist movement, of which it is totally independent. As for ourselves, we arrived at this proposition before we became acquainted with Marx, to whose influence we have in no way been subjected. This is because this conception is the logical extension of the entire historical and psychological movement of the last fifty years. For a long time past, historians have perceived that social evolution has causes with which the authors of historical events are unacquainted. It is under the influence of these ideas that they tend to deny or to restrict the role of great men and look to literary, legal, and other movements for the expression of a collective thought which no specific personality completely incarnates. At the same time and above all, individual psychology taught us that the individual's consciousness very often merely reflects the underlying state of the organism and that the current of our representations is determined by causes of which the subject is unaware. It was then natural to extend this conception to collective psychology. But we are not able to perceive what part the sad class conflict which we are presently witnessing could have played in the elaboration or the development of this idea. No doubt, the idea came at a fitting time, when the conditions necessary for its appearance were present. It would not have been possible in just any era. But the question is to know what these conditions are, and when Labriola affirms that it has been roused "by the ample, conscious and continuous development of modern technology, by the inevitable suggestion of a new world which is being born," he takes as self-evident a thesis without proof. Socialism has been able to employ the idea to its advantage, but it has not produced it, and, above all, it does not imply it.

It is true that if, as our author postulates, this objective conception of history were just the same as the doctrine of economic materialism, then, since the latter certainly has socialist origins, one might believe that the former was constituted under the same influence and inspired by the same spirit. *But this confusion is devoid of all foundation, and it is important to bring it to an end.* There is no interdependence between these two theories, the scientific value of which is singularly unequal. Just as it seems true to us that the causes of social phenomena must be sought outside individual representations, it seems to that same degree false that they can be reduced, in the final analysis, to the state of industrial technology, and that the economic factor is the mainspring of progress.

Even without opposing any definite fact to economic materialism, how could one help but notice the insufficiency of the proofs on which it rests? Here is a law which pretends to be the key to history! To demonstrate it, a few sparse, disjointed facts are cited, facts which do not constitute any methodical series and the interpretation of which is far from being settled: primitive communism, the struggles of the patricians and plebians, of the common people and the nobility, are advanced as having economic explanations. Even when a few examples borrowed from the industrial history of England are added to these rare documents, rapidly passed in review, they will not have succeeded in demonstrating a generalization of such magnitude. On this issue Marxism is at variance with its own principle. It begins by declaring that social life depends upon causes which escape awareness and conscious reason. But then, in order to get at these causes, one would have to employ procedures at least as indirect and at least as complex as those used in the natural sciences; all sorts of observations, experiments, and laborious comparisons would be necessary to discover a few of these factors in isolation, let alone to attempt to obtain at present a single representation of them. And here we are, in a twinkling, with all these mysteries clarified and with a simple solution to these problems which human intelligence appeared so hard pressed to penetrate! Could we not say that the objective conception which we have just summarily set forth has not been proved in an adequate way? Nothing is surer. But what is more, it does not propose to assign a definite origin to social phenomena; it limits itself to affirming that they have causes. For, to say that they have objective causes has no other meaning, since collective representations cannot have their causes in themselves. It is, therefore, simply a postulate intended to direct research and, consequently, forever suspect, for it is experience which must decide in the final analysis. It is a rule of method, not a law from which one is authorized to deduce important consequences, either theoretical or practical.

Not only is the Marxist hypothesis unproved, but it is contrary to facts which seem well established. Sociologists and historians tend more and more to meet in the confirmation that religion is the most primitive of all social phenomena. From it, by successive transformations, have come all the other manifestations of collective activity: law, ethics, art, science, political forms, and so on. Everything is religious in principle. We know of no way to reduce religion to economics, nor of any attempt to accomplish this reduction. No one has yet shown under what economic influences naturism arose out of totemism, as a result of what modifications in technology it became the abstract monotheism of Jahweh in one place and the Greco-Latin polytheism in another; we strongly doubt that anyone will ever succeed in such an enterprise. More generally, it is indisputable that in the beginning the economic factor is rudimentary while religious life is, on the contrary, rich and overwhelming. How then could the latter result from the former, and is it not probable, on the contrary, that the economy depends on religion much more than the second on the first?

The preceding ideas, moreover, must not be pushed to an extreme where they lose all validity. Psycho-physiology, after pointing to the organic substratum as the basis of all psychic life, has often committed the error of refusing all reality to the latter; the resulting theory reduces consciousness to nothing but an epiphenomenon. We have lost from view the fact that, although representations originally depend on organic states, once they are constituted, they are, by that very fact, realities sui generis, autonomous and capable of being causes in turn, capable of producing new phenomena. Sociology must carefully refrain from making the same error. While the different forms of collective activity also have their own substratum, and while they derive from it in the last instance, once they exist, they become, in turn, creative sources of action, they have an effectiveness all their own, and they react on the very causes on which they depend. We are, therefore, far from maintaining that the economic factor is only an epiphenomenon: once it exists, it has an influence which is special to it; it can partially modify the very substratum from which it results. But we have no reason to confuse it, in some way, with this substratum and to make of it something particularly fundamental. Everything leads us to believe, on the contrary, that it is secondary and derived. From which it follows that the economic transformations which have occurred in the course of this century – the substitution of large-scale for small-scale industry – in no way necessitate an overthrow and an integral renewal of the social order, and even that the malaise from which European societies may suffer need not have these transformations as their cause.

Part Two

Division of Labour, Crime and Punishment

THE DIVISION OF LABOUR IN SOCIETY

Preface to the first edition

This work originated with the question about the relationship between individual personality and social solidarity. How can it be that the individual, while becoming more autonomous, depends more heavily on society? How can he be at the same time both more individual and more socially integrated? It is undeniable that these two movements, contradictory though they may appear, develop along parallel lines That was the problem we raised: it seemed that what resolved this apparent dichotomy was a change in social solidarity brought about by the ever-increasing development of the division of labour. This is what led us to make it the object of our study.

INTRODUCTION

The Problem

Although the division of labour is not new, it was only at the end of the eighteenth century that societies began to be aware of the principle to which, until then, they had been subject almost unwittingly. To be sure, even from antiquity, several thinkers recognized its importance, but Adam Smith was the first to attempt a theory of it. It was he who invented the term that social science subsequently lent to biology.

From: *De la Division du travail social*, Paris, Alcan, 1893. Translation by Margaret Thompson.

This phenomenon is so widespread today that it is immediately obvious to everyone. No longer can we have any illusions about the direction of modern industry: it tends to develop more powerful machinery, large concentrations of forces and capital, and therefore an extreme division of labour. Not only are occupations separated and specialized *ad infinitum* within factories, but each product is itself a speciality which presupposes others. Adam Smith and Stuart Mill still hoped that agriculture, at least, would be the exception to the rule, and they saw it as the last refuge of small-scale ownership. Although one should be careful not to generalize unduly in such matters, it does, nevertheless, seem difficult to deny today that the main branches of agricultural industry are increasingly being drawn into this general movement. Finally, business itself is ingeniously and subtly responding to and reflecting the infinite diversity of industrial enterprises. While this evolution occurs in an unplanned and spontaneous way, economists who examine its causes and analyse its results, far from condemning or opposing it, maintain it to be necessary. They see it as reflecting a higher law of human societies and as the requirement for their progress.

But the division of labour is not peculiar to the economic world; its growing influence can be observed in quite different sectors of society. Political, administrative, and judicial functions are increasingly specialized. The same is true for artistic and scientific functions. We are far removed from the time when philosophy was the only science; it has been fragmented into mutlitude of specialized disciplines, each of which has its own object, method and thought. 'With each passing era, men who have made their mark in the sciences have become increasingly specialized.'

[. . .]

BOOK I: THE FUNCTION OF THE DIVISION OF LABOUR
METHOD FOR DETERMINING THIS FUNCTION

But how do we proceed to verification?

It is not sufficient simply to investigate if, i nthese sorts of societies, there exists a social solidarity which is produced by the division of labour. This is a self-evident truth, since in such societies the division of labour is highly developed and produces solidarity. We must determine rather to what extent the solidarity that it produces contributes to the general integration of the society: for it is only then that we shall know how necessary it is, and if it is indeed an essential factor for social cohesion, or, on the contrary, whether it is merely an accessory or secondary condition. In order to answer this question, we must compare this social link with others, so that we can measure its part in the total effect. To do this we must begin by classifying the different types of social solidarity.

But the social solidarity is a completely moral phenomenon which in itself does not lend itself to precise observation nor indeed to measurement. In order to carry out a classification and comparison we have to substitute for this elusive, internal fact, an external index which symbolizes it, and then study the former by means of the latter.

This visible symbol is law. In fact, wherever social solidarity exists, despite its immaterial quality, it manifests its presence by palpable effects, rather than remaining in a state of pure potentiality. Wherever it is strong, it pushes men together, puts them in frequent contact, and increases their opportunities to enter into relationships with each other. At this point, it is difficult to say whether the social solidarity produces these phenomena or whether it is the result of them; whether men become close because it is a driving force, or whether it is a driving force because they have entered into relationships with each other. But, for the moment, it is not necessary to elucidate this question; it is sufficient to note that these two orders of facts are linked and vary at the same time and in the same direction. The more socially integrated the members of a society are, the more they sustain diverse relations, either with each other or with the group taken collectively: for, if their encounters were rare, they would be mutually dependent only inter-mittently and tenuously. On the other hand, the number of these relationships is necessarily proportional to the number of juridicial rules which determine them. Indeed, wherever social life has a durable existence, it inevitably tends to assume a precise form and to be organized, and the law is nothing other than this very organization in its most stable, most precise form. The general life of the society cannot be extended unless the juridicial life is extended at the same time and in direct relation to it. We can thus be sure of finding all the essential varieties of social solidarity reflected in the law.

It might be argued that social relations can become fixed without assuming a juridicial form. Sometimes their regulation does not attain this degree of consolidation or precision; but they do not remain indeterminate for that reason: instead of being regulated by law they are regulated by custom. Law, then, reflects only a part of social life, and, consequently, provides us only with incomplete data for resolving the problem. Furthermore, it often happens that custom is not in accord with the law; it is constantly being said that custom tempers the rigours of the law, that it mitigates excessive formalism, and sometimes even that it is inspired by a completely different spirit. Might it not be the case that custom manifests other sorts of social solidarity than that expressed in positive law?

But this opposition arises only in quite exceptional circumstances. This happens when law no longer corresponds to the present state of the society, yet is maintained without apparent reason, by force of habit. In this case, new relationships which are established in spite of it, cannot avoid becoming organized, for they cannot last without seeking consolidation. But since they are in conflict with the old existing law, they do not go beyond the stage of custom and do not manage to enter juridicial life proper. It is in this way that conflict erupts. But it can only arise in rare and pathological cases, which cannot persist without being dangerous. Normally, custom is not opposed to law but is, on the contrary, its very basis. It is true that sometimes nothing develops from this basis. Social relationships may exist which require only the diffuse regulation that comes from custom; but this is because they lack importance and continuity, except, of course, in the abnormal cases just referred to. So, if there are types of social solidarity that custom alone reveals, they are certainly very secondary; by contrast, law reproduces all the essential types, and these are the only ones that we need to know about.

Shall we go further and say that social solidarity is not entirely manifested in a tangible way, that these manifestations are only partial and imperfect, and that beyond law and custom there is an internal state from whence it derives, and that to know it truly, we must get to its essence and without intermediaries? But we can know causes scientifically only by the effects that they produce, and in order to better determine their nature, science chooses from the effects those which are the most objective and which lend themselves best to measurement. Science studies heat through variations in the volume of bodies produced by changes in temperature, electricity through physical and chemical effects, and force through movement. Why should social solidarity be an exception?

What remains of it once divested of its social forms? It is the nature of the group whose unity it assures that gives it its specific characteristics: this is why it varies according to the social types. The same social solidarity does not exist in the family as in political societies; we are not attached to our country in the same way that the Roman was attached to his city or the Hun to his tribe. But since these differences are related to social causes, we can understand them only through the differences that the social effects of solidarity produce. So if we neglect these differences, all the variations become indiscernible and we can no longer perceive what is common to all of them, namely, the general tendency to sociability, a tendency which is always and everywhere the same, and is not related to any particular social type. But this residue is merely an abstraction, for sociability in itself is not to be found anywhere. What do exist and in dynamic ways are the particular forms of solidarity: domestic solidarity, professional solidarity, national solidarity, yesterday's, today's, etc. Each one has its own nature; consequently, these generalizations provide only a very incomplete explanation of the phenomenon, since they necessarily leave out what is concrete and dynamic.

Thus the study of solidarity depends on sociology. It is a social fact that we can understand only through the intermediary of its social effects. Many moralists and psychologists have been able to deal with the question without following this method, because they have evaded the difficulty. They have eliminated everything that is peculiarly social from the phenomenon in order to retain only the psychological germ from which it developed. For it is certainly the case that solidarity, while being a social fact of the first order, depends on our individual organism. In order to exist, it must be contained within our physical and psychological constitution. At a pinch one might be content with studying this aspect of it. But, in that case, one sees only its least distinct, least special part. This is not even solidarity proper, but rather that element which makes it possible.

Moreover, this abstract study would not be very fertile in results. For, if solidarity remains merely as a disposition of our psychological nature, it is too indefinate to be easily comprehended. It is an intangible phenomenon which does not lend itself to observation. In order to assume a comprehensible form, it must undergo an overt translation into certain social consequences. Moreover, even in this indeterminate state, it depends on social conditions which give rise to it, and from which, consequently, it cannot be detached. This is why it is rare for these purely psychological analyses not to be mixed in with certain sociological views. For example, we speak of the influence of the gregarious state on the formation of social sentiment in general; or else we give a quick indication of the principal social relations in which sociability most obviously depends. Certainly these additional considerations, introduced haphazardly by way of examples and chance suggestions, would not be sufficient to elucidate the social nature of solidarity. At least they demonstrate that the sociological perspective is required even of psychologists.

Our method is now fully outlined. Since law reproduces the principal forms of social solidarity, we have only to classify the different types of law in order to discover which are the different, corresponding types of social solidarity. It is already likely that there is a type which symbolizes the special solidarity brought about by the division of labour. Once found, it will be sufficient to compare the number of juridical rules expressing it to the total volume of the law, in order to measure the part played by the division of labour.

For this task, we cannot use the distinctions made by legal experts. Created for practical purposes, they can be very convenient from that point of view, but science cannot be satisfied with these empirical and approximate classifications. The most widespread is the classification into public and private law; public law is supposed to regulate relationships between the individual and the state, and private law between individuals. But when one looks more closely at these terms, the demarcation line, at first glance seemingly clear, begins to disappear. All law is private, in the sense that it is always and everywhere concerned with individuals who are both present and acting; but all law is primarily public, in the sense that it is a social function, and that all individuals are, in different ways, functionaries of society. [. . .] And what is the State? Where does it begin and end? We know how controversial the question is: it is not scientific to base a fundamental classification on a notion so obscure and so badly analysed.

To proceed methodically, we have to find some characteristic which is both essential to juridical phenomena and is likely to vary when they vary. Every legal precept can be defined as a rule of conduct which is sanctioned. On the other hand, it is clear that sanctions change according to the seriousness attributed to the precepts, the place that they occupy in the public consciousness, and the role that they play in society. It is therefore appropriate to classify juridical rules according to the different sanctions attached to them.

There are two kinds. The first consists essentially of imposing some suffering, or at least some disadvantage, upon the offender; the purpose is to diminish his fortune, his honour, his life, or his freedom, to deprive him of something that he enjoys. These are said to be repressive sanctions: this is penal law. It is true that those sanctions related to purely moral rules have the same characteristic; but these sanctions are distributed in a diffuse manner, by everybody indiscriminately, whilst penal law sanctions are applied only through the intermediary of a particular organ: they are organized. The second kind of sanction does not necessarily involve suffering on the part of the offender, but consists only of *restoring the previous state of affairs,* of re-establishing relationships that have been disturbed to their normal state. This is done either by forcibly restoring the impugned act to the type from which it deviated, or by annulling it, by depriving it of all social value. We must therefore divide juridical rules into two major classes, depending on whether they have organized repressive sanctions, or purely restitutive sanctions. The first class includes all penal law; the second, civil law, commercial law, procedural law, administrative and constitutional law, after allowing for the penal rule that may be found in them.

Let us now investigate the kind of social solidarity which corresponds to each of these types.

MECHANICAL SOLIDARITY BASED ON LIKENESS

The totality of beliefs and sentiments common to average members of the same society forms a particular system with a life of its own; one might call it the collective or common consciousness. It is true that it does not have a substratum in a specific organ; by definition, it is diffused throughout the whole of society; nevertheless, it does have specific characteristics which make it a distinctive reality. In fact, it is independent of the particular conditions in which individuals are situated. They come and go, but it remains. It is the same in the north and the south, in large cities and small towns, and in different professions. Similarly, it does not change with each generation, but, on the contrary, it links generations. It is, therefore, something completely different from individual consciousnesses, even though it is materialized only through individuals. It is the psychological life of society, one which has its own properties, conditions of existence and mode of development, just as individuals do, but in a different way. For this reason, it is entitled to be designated by a special term. The word that we have used above is not without ambiguity. As the terms 'collective' and 'social' are often considered synonymous, one is inclined to believe that the collective consciousness is the total social consciousness, that is, that the collective consciousness includes the whole psychological life of society, whereas it is only a very small part of it, especially in advanced societies. Judicial, governmental, scientific and industrial functions, in short, all specialized functions, are of a psychological order, since they consist of systems of representations and actions; however, they are clearly outside the common consciousness. To avoid confusion, the best thing would be to create a technical expression that would specifically designate the whole complex of shared social characteristics. However, since the use of a new word when it is not absolutely necessary has its drawbacks, we shall retain the well-established expression 'collective or common consciousness', but always bear in mind the narrow sense in which we are using it.

Summarizing the previous analysis, we can say that an act is criminal when it offends strong and defined states of the collective consciousness.

The literal meaning of this proposition is rarely questioned, but usually it takes on a very different meaning from what it should have. It is taken to express not the essential characteristics of crime, but one of its repercussions. We know that crime offends against widely-held, intense feelings; but it is believed that this pervasiveness and intensity spring from the criminal nature of the act, which consequently still remains to be defined. It is not disputed that every criminal act meets with universal disapproval, but it tends to be taken for granted that the disapproval results from its offensiveness. But one is hard put to say what this offensiveness consists of. Does it consist of a particularly serious immorality? I wish it were so; but this is to answer one question by posing another, by playing with words. For it is precisely the problem to know what immorality is, and particularly this immorality that society represses by means of a system of punishments, and which constitutes criminality. Obviously, it can only derive from one or more characteristics that are common to all types of criminality; the only characteristic that might satisfy this condition is the opposition that exists between the crime, whatever it may be, and certain collective sentiments. It is, therefore, this opposition that determines what is crime, rather than arising as an effect of it. In other words, we must not say that an act offends the common consciousness because it is criminal, but that it is criminal because it offends the common consciousness. We do not condemn it because it is a crime, but it is a crime because we condemn it. It is impossible to be specific about the intrinsic nature of these sentiments: they are directed at widely different objects, and cannot be encompassed within a single formula. They cannot be said to relate to the vital interests of society, nor to a minimum of justice; all of these definitions are inadequate. There is only one way of recognizing it: it is a sentiment, whatever its origin and purpose, that is found in all consciousnesses, endowed with a certain degree of force and precision, and every act which offends against it is a crime. [. . .]

However, there are some cases where the preceding explanation does not apply. There are some acts which are more severely repressed than the degree of condemnation they receive from public opinion. Thus, conspiracy among public officials, the encroachment of the judiciary on administrative authorities, or by religious upon secular functions, these are the object of a repression which is not commensurate with the indignation they arouse in individual consciousnesses.

The removal of official documents leaves us quite indifferent and yet is punished rather severely. It may even be the case that the punished act does not directly offend any collective sentiment: there is nothing within us that protests against fishing and hunting out of season, or allowing over-loaded vehicles on the public highway. Yet there is no reason to separate completely these offences from others; any radical distinction would be arbitrary, since they all manifest the same external criterion to varying degrees. Certainly, in none of these examples does the punishment appear unjust; if it were contrary to custom, it could not have been established. But although it is not rejected by public opinion, such opinion, if left to itself, would either not demand the punishment at all, or would show itself to be less demanding. So, in all cases of this type, the degree of criminality does not derive, or at least not completely, from the strength of the collective sentiments that are offended, but rather from some other cause.

It is certainly the case that once some governmental authority becomes established, it has in itself enough power to attach penal sanctions to certain rules of conduct. By its own action it is capable of creating certain offences or of increasing the seriousness of other crimes. Furthermore, all the acts referred to have the common characteristic that they are directed against one of the bodies that control social life. Must we therefore accept that there are two types of crime arising from two different causes? Such a hypothesis should not be considered. However numerous are the varieties of crime, it is always essentially the same, since it always produces the same effect — punishment; this does not change its nature, even though it may vary in intensity. The same fact cannot have two causes, unless this duality is only apparent and the two causes are basically the same. So the State's power to react must be the same as the power diffused throughout society.

Where could this come from? Is it from the importance of the interests that are under the direction of the State, which require special protection? But we know that even harm caused to important interests is not in itself sufficient to determine the penal response; the harm must be perceived in a particular way. How does it come about that the slight harm to a governmental body is punished, whereas redress for much more serious damage to other social bodies is brought about through civil action? The smallest infraction of highway control is punished by a fine, but even frequently repreated violations of contracts, or constant unscrupulousness in economic relations, only require the payment of damages. Certainly the system of governmental direction plays an important part in social life, but there are other systems with important interests, yet their functioning is not protected in this way. The brain is important, but the stomach is also essential, and illness in either is a threat to life. Why is this privileged position given to what is sometimes referred to as the social brain?

The problem is easily solved if we draw attention to the fact that, wherever a governing authority is established, its first and main function is to create respect for collective beliefs, traditions and practices; that is, to defend the common consciousness against all enemies, both internal and external. It thus becomes the symbol of the collective consciousness, its living expression in everyone's eyes. Thus, the vitality of the common consciousness is transmitted to the governing authority, in the same way that affinities of ideas are communicated through the words which express them. This is how the governing authority acquires a character which puts it in a paramount position. It is no longer one among many important social functions; it is the collectivity incarnate. It participates in the authority that the latter exercises over individual consciousnesses, and it is from the collective consciousness that it derives its power. But, once this power is established, without becoming independent of the source from which it flows and from which it continues to draw sustenance, it becomes an autonomous factor in social life, capable of spontaneous actions not determined by outside forces, precisely as a result of its acquired supremacy. However, since it is only a derivative of the force immanent in the collective consciousness, it therefore has the same properties and reactions, even when the collective consciousness does not react completely in unison. It therefore reacts against all forces that are opposed to it, as would the more diffused consciousness of society, even though the latter does not experience the opposition, or at least not as directly. In other words, it regards acts as criminal if they offend it, even if they do not offend the collective sentiments to the same degree. But it is from these collective sentiments that it receives all its power to create crimes and offences. Aside from the fact that the power could not come from elsewhere, or out of nothing, the following facts, which will be developed at length in the rest of this book, confirm this explanation. The extent of the action of the governmental authority in determining the number and type of criminal acts depends on the power it can draw on. This in turn can be measured either by the extent of the authority it exercises over its citizens, or by the degree of seriousness attached to crimes directed against it. We shall see that in less developed societies this authority and the degree of seriousness are much greater, and furthermore, the collective consciousness has most power in societies of that type.

Thus it is always to the collective consciousness that we shall return: all criminality flows from this, either directly or indirectly. Crime is not simply damage done to interests, even if they are serious; it is an offence against an authority that is in some way transcendent. But we know from experience that there is no moral force superior to the individual, except collective moral force.

There is a way of verifying this conclusion. What characterizes a crime is that it determines the punishment. Consequently, if our definition of crime is correct, it must explain all the characteristics of the punishment. [. . .]

Firstly, punishment consists of an emotional reaction. This characteristic is particularly apparent in less cultivated societies. In effect, primitive peoples punish for the sake of punishing, making the guilty person suffer simply so that he might experience suffering, without expecting to gain any advantage themselves from the suffering they inflict. [. . .] But it is said that nowadays punishment has changed its character; it is no longer to avenge itself that society punishes, it is to defend itself. In its hands, the pain that it inflicts is nothing more than a methodical means for its own protection. It punishes not because the punishment itself offers any satisfaction, but in order that the fear of punishment may deter the potential wrongdoer. It is no longer anger that determines repression, but calculating foresight. Thus our earlier comments could not be applied more generally; they would only apply to the primitive form of punishment and could not be extended to the existing form.

But to justify such a radical distinction between these two sorts of punishment, it is not enough to show that they are employed for different ends. The nature of a practice does not necessarily change because the conscious intentions of those who apply it are modified. [. . .] It adapts itself to new conditions of existence without undergoing any essential changes. This is so in the case of punishment. [. . .] And indeed, punishment has remained, at least in part, an act of vengeance. It is said that we do not make the guilty undergo suffering for its own sake; but it is nonetheless true that we deem it right that he should suffer. We may be wrong to do so, but that is not the issue. [. . .] The proof of this lies in the detailed precautions we take to make sure the punishment matches as closely as possible the seriousness of the crime. The efforts would be inexplicable if we did not believe the guilty person ought to suffer because he has done wrong, and should suffer in proportion to that wrong. In fact, this gradation is unnecessary if punishment is only a means of defence. [. . .] Thus punishment remains for us what it was to our predecessors. It is still an act of vengeance, since it is an expiation. What we avenge, and what the criminal expiates, is the outrage to morality. [. . .] We can therefore state that punishment consists of a passionate reaction of graduated intensity. [. . .]

Thus the analysis of punishment confirms our definition of crime. We began by establishing inductively that crime consisted essentially of an act contrary to strong and defined states of the common consciousness. We have just seen that all the characteristics of punishment derive from the nature of crime. This is because the rules for which punishment acts as a sanction express the most essential social similarities.

In this way we can see what kind of solidarity penal law symbolizes. We all know that there is a social cohesion whose cause lies in a certain conformity of individual consciousness to a common type, which is none other than the psychological life of the society. In these conditions, not only are all the members of the group individually attracted to each other because they share a common resemblance, but they are also attached to what is the condition for the existence of this collective type, that is, to the society that they form by their union. Not only do citizens like each other and seek each other out in preference to foreigners, but they also love their country. Its needs are their needs, they are dependent on its persistence and prosperity, because without it, a large part of their psychological life would be hampered. Conversely, society depends on what they have to offer on the basis of their shared basic characteristics, because this is a condition of its own cohesion. There are, within each of us, two consciousnesses: one contains only states that are personal to each one of us, our individual characteristics, whilst the other consists of states which are common throughout society.[1] The former represents only our individual personality, which it constitutes; the latter represents the collective type and consequently the society without which it could not exist. When it is one of the elements of the latter that determines our conduct, we do not act in our own personal interest, but in the pursuit of collective ends. Although distinct, these two consciousness are linked to each other since, in effect, they are as one, possessing the same organic basis. Thus they are solidly joined together. From this there results a solidarity *sui generis* which, deriving from the shared characteristics, directly links the individual to society. In the next chapter we will be in a better position to show why we suggest calling it 'mechanical'. This solidarity

---

[1] In order to simplify this explanation we are assuming that the individual belongs to only one society. In fact, we participate in several groups and there is in each of us several collective consciousnesses. But this complication does not change the relationship that we are discussing.

consists not only in a general and indeterminate attachment of the individual to the group, but it also makes all individual detailed actions harmonious. In fact, as these collective impulses are everywhere the same, they always produce the same effects. Consequently, every time they are brought into play, all wills move spontaneously and together in the same direction.

It is mechanical solidarity that is expressed in repressive law, at least with regard to its vital elements. In practice, the acts that such law prohibits and labels as crimes are of two sorts: either they directly manifest too much of a violent contrast between the characteristics of the offender and those of the collective type, or else they offend against the organ of the common consciousness. In both cases, the force that is offended by the crime and suppresses it, is the same. It is a product of the most vital social similarities and it has the result of maintaining the social cohesion which derives from these similarities. It is this force that penal law protects against being undermined, both by requiring from each of us a minimum of similarities, without which the individual would be a threat to the unity of the social body, and by imposing respect for that which symbolizes and expresses those similarities. [. . .]

The same is true for punishment. Although it proceeds from a totally mechanical reaction, from passionate emotions that are largely unthinking, this does not prevent it from playing a useful role. But this role is not the one that we ordinarily perceive. It does not serve, or only in a very secondary way, to correct the guilty person or to deter potential imitators. With regard to both of these its effectiveness is quite rightly doubted, and it is in any case weak. Its real function is to maintain social cohesion intact by preserving the vitality of the common consciousness. [. . .]

Thus, we can say, without being paradoxical, that punishment is above all designed to act upon law-abiding people. For, since it serves to heal wounds inflicted upon the collective sentiments, it can only fulfil this role where such sentiments exist and to the extent that they are active. [. . .]

The conclusion of this chapter is that there exists a social solidarity which derives from the fact that a certain number of states of consciousness are common to all members of the same society. It is this social solidarity that repressive law materially embodies, at least in its essential elements. The part that it plays in the general integration of society obviously depends on the extent of the area of social life included in, and regulated by, the common consciousness. The more varied the relations where the common consciousness makes itself felt, and the more links it creates attaching the individual to the group, then the more social cohesion will derive completely from this cause and bear its imprint. But the number of these relations is itself proportional to the number of repressive rules. By determining what proportion of the judicial system is represented by penal law, we shall at the same time measure the relative importance of this solidarity.

ORGANIC SOLIDARITY DUE TO THE DIVISION OF LABOUR

The actual nature of the restitutive sanction is sufficient to demonstrate that the social solidarity to which this type of law corresponds is totally different.

This sanction is distinguished by the fact that it is not expiatory, but consists simply of a return to a previous state. Suffering in proportion to the misdeed is not inflicted on the one who has violated or disregarded the law; he is simply ordered to comply with it. If certain actions were committed, the judge reinstates them to the way they were before. He talks about law; but he says nothing about punishment. Payments of damages do not have a penal character; they are merely a means of reviewing the past in order to restore it, as far as possible, to its normal condition. [. . .]

While repressive law tends to remain diffuse within society, restitutive law creates organs which are increasingly specialized: consultative tribunals, arbitration councils, administrative tribunals of all kinds. Even in its most general aspect, relating to civil law, it is exercised solely through specific functionaries: magistrate, lawyers, etc., who have become qualified in this role because of very specialized training.

But, although these rules are relatively external to the collective consciousness, they are not solely concerned with individuals. If this were the case, restitutive law would have no connection with social solidarity, for the relations it regulates would bind individuals to each other without binding them to society. They would simply be occurrences in private life, in the same way as friendly relationships are. But society is far from being uninvolved in this sphere of juridical life. It is true that, on the whole, it does not intervene directly and on its own initiative; it has to be invited by the interested parties. But, when it is called upon, its intervention is nevertheless the essential driving force, since it alone can make the system function. It sets forth the law through the agency of its representatives. [. . .]

Since negative solidarity in itself does not bring about any integration and since, moreover, there is nothing specific about it, we shall recognize only two sorts of positive solidarity, distinguishable by the following characteristics:

(1) The first kind links the individual directly to society without any intermediary. With the second kind, the individual depends on society, because he depends on the parts which make the whole.

(2) Society is not viewed in the same way in the two cases. In the first case, what we call society is a more or less organized totality of beliefs and sentiments common to all the members of the group: this is the collective type. On the other hand, the society in which we are integrated in the second case is a system of different, special functions which are linked by precise relationships. These two societies are but one. They are two faces of one and the same reality, but which none the less need to be distinguished.

(3) Out of this second difference there arises another which will help us to describe and name these two sorts of solidarity.

The first kind can be strong only to the extent that the ideas and inclinations common to all the members of the society are greater in number and intensity than those which belong personally to each of them; the greater the excess, the stronger the solidarity. Now, our personality is made up of everything that is peculiar to and characteristic of us, everything that distinguishes it from others. This solidarity can, therefore, only increase in inverse proportion to the personality. As we have said, there are in the consciousness of each of us two consciousnesses: one which is common to our whole group, which, consequently, is not ourselves, but is society living and acting within us; the other represents us at our most personal and distinctive, in everything that makes us an individual. The solidarity that derives from similarities is at its maximum when the collective consciousness completely envelops our total consciousness and coincides with it at every point: but, at that moment, our individuality is nil. Our individuality can come into being only if the community takes up less place within us. There are two contrary forces, one centripetal, the other centrifugal, which cannot both increase at the same time. We cannot develop at the same time in two such opposing directions. If we have a strong inclination to think and act for ourselves, we cannot also be strongly inclined to think and act like others. If the ideal is to make a distinct, personal character for oneself, then it would not be ideal to resemble everyone else. Furthermore, at the very moment when this solidarity exercises its influence, our personality collapses, one might say, by definition; for we are no longer ourselves; we are a collective being.

The social molecules which would cohere only in this way could act together only to the extent that they have no movements of their own, as do molecules in inorganic bodies. This is why we suggest calling this type of solidarity 'mechanical'. The word does not imply that it is produced by mechanical, artificial means. We only use this term by analogy to the cohesion which unites the elements of raw materials, as opposed to the cohesion which brings about the unity of living bodies. What justifies this term is that the link which binds the individual to society is wholly analogous to the link between a thing and a person. Individual consciousness, considered from this viewpoint, is simply dependent on the collective type and follows all its movements, in the same way as the possessed object follows those required by its owner. In societies where his solidarity is highly developed, the individual is not his own master, as we shall see later, quite literally, he is a thing at the disposal of the society. Also in these same social types, personal rights are not yet distinguished from real rights.

The solidarity produced by the division of labour is quite different. Whereas the preceding type implies that individuals resemble each other, this type assumes that they are different from each other. The first is possible only to the extent that the individual personality is absorbed into the collective personality; the second is possible only if each has its own sphere of action, and therefore a personality. The collective consciousness must therefore leave open a part of the individual consciousness, so that these special functions which it cannot regulate may be established; the more this area is extended, the stronger is the cohesion which results from its solidarity. In fact, on the one hand, the more labour is divided up, the greater the dependence on society, and, on the other hand, the more specialized the activity of each individual, the more personal it is. Circumscribed though that activity may be, it is never completely original; even in the exercise of our profession, we conform to usages and practices which are common to the entire professional body. But, even in this case, the burden that we accept is less heavy than when the whole of society weighs on us, and it leaves much more room for the free play of our initiative. So, the individuality of the whole increases at the same time as the individuality of its parts; the society becomes more capable of collective movement, at the same time as each of its elements has more freedom of movement of its own. This resembles the solidarity that is observed in higher animals. Each organ, in fact, has its special characteristics, its autonomy, and yet, the greater the unity of the organism, the more marked is the individuation of its parts. Using this analogy, we propose to call the solidarity due to the division of labour 'organic'.

THE INCREASING PREPONDERANCE OF ORGANIC SOLIDARITY AND ITS CONSEQUENCES

If there is one truth that history has settled beyond all question, it is that religion embraces an ever-diminishing part of social life. Originally it extended to everything; everything social was religious; the two words were synonymous. Then gradually political, economic and scientific functions freed themselves from the religious function, became established separately, taking on an increasingly pronounced temporal character. God, if we may express it in this way, at first present in all human relationships, gradually withdrew from them; he abandoned the world to men and their disputes. At least, if he did continue to dominate it, it was from on high and at a distance, and the influence which he exercised, becoming more general and imprecise, left more room for the free play of human forces. The individual feels himself to be, and is, in fact, less 'acted upon'; he becomes more a source of spontaneous activity. In short, not only does the sphere of religion not increase at the same time and to the same extent as the sphere of temporal life, but it progressively diminishes. This regression did not begin at a precise moment in history, but one can follow its phases going back to the origins of social evolution. It is therefore bound up with the fundamental conditions of the development of societies, and it thus demonstrates that there is an ever-decreasing number of collective beliefs and sentiments which are both sufficiently collective and strong to assume a religious character. This means that the average intensity of the common consciousness progressively weakens.

This demonstration has one advantage over the previous one; it allows us to establish that the same law of regression applies just as much to the representative element of the common consciousness as to the affective element. Through the penal law, we can only get at phenomena relating to sensibilities, whilst religion covers ideas and doctrines as well as sentiments.

The decrease in the number of proverbs, adages, sayings, etc., as societies develop, is further proof that collective representations also become progressively less well defined.

ORGANIC AND CONTRACTUAL SOLIDARITY

The following propositions summarize the first part of this work.

Social life derives from a dual source, the similarity of consciousnesses and the social division of labour. In the first case the individual is socialized because, in the absence of any real individuality, he is united with others with whom he shares a common likeness, becoming part of the same collective type; in the second case, because, while having an appearance and personal activity which distinguish him from others, he is dependent on them to the same extent that he is distinguished from them, and consequently upon the society which results from this combination.

The similarity of consciousnesses produces juridical rules accompanied by the threat of repressive sanctions which impose uniform beliefs and practices on everyone. The more marked this tendency is, the more completely is social life identified with religious life, and the more communist are economic institutions.

The division of labour produces juridical rules which govern the nature and relations of divided functions, but their violation elicits only restitutive sanctions which do not have an expiatory character.

Each of these sets of juridical rules is also accompanied by a set of purely moral injunctions. Where penal law is very extensive, common morality is also widespread; in other words, there is a whole host of collective practices that are protected by public opinion. Where restitutive law is highly developed, each profession has its own occupational morality. [. . .] Profession misdemeanours are much more mildly rebuked than attacks against public morality. However, rules concerning occupational morality and justices are just as imperative as others. They compel the individual to act with a view to ends which are not strictly his own, to make concessions, to agree to compromises, to take into account higher interests than his own. Consequently, even where society is most completely dependent on the division of labour, it is not reduced to a collection of juxtaposed atoms, among which it can establish only external, temporary contacts. On the contrary, the members are united by ties which extend deeper and further than the brief periods of exchanges. Each of their functions is performed in a fixed way, dependent upon others, and forms a solidary system with them. Consequently, permanent duties arise out of the nature of the chosen task. Because we fulfil a specific domestic or social function, we are involved in a complex of obligations from which we have no right to free ourselves. There exists one organ, above all, upon which we are increasingly dependent – the State. The points of contact with it multiply as do the occasions when it is given the task of evoking the sentiment of common solidarity.

BOOK II: THE CAUSES AND CONDITIONS

THE CAUSES

The division of labour develops, therefore, to the extent that there are more individuals in sufficient contact to be able to act and react upon one another. If we can agree to call this relation and the active commerce that results 'dynamic or moral density', it can be said that the progress of the division of labour is in direct ratio to the moral or dynamic density of society.

But this moral relationship can have its effect only if the actual distance between individuals has itself diminished in some way. Moral density cannot increase unless material density grows at the same time, and the latter can be used to measure the former. It is pointless to attempt to discover which determined the other; they cannot be separated.

The increased density of societies develops historically in three main ways:

(1) Whereas the population of lower societies is spread widely over large areas, in more advanced societies, the population always tends to be concentrated. [. . .]

(2) The creation and development of cities is an even more characteristic indication of the same phenomenon. [. . .]

(3) Finally, there is the factor of the number and rapidity of methods of communication and transportation. [. . .]

If the concentration of society has this result it is because it multiplies intra-social relations. But these will be even more numerous if the total number of members of the population also increases. If it consists of more individuals as well as closer contacts, the effect must be reinforced. Social volume, therefore, has the same effect as density upon the division of labour. [. . .]

Thus we can formulate the following proposition: *The division of labour varies in direct ratio with the volume and density of societies, and, if it progresses in a continuous way throughout the course of social development, it is because societies regularly became denser and generally increase in volume.*

[. . .] If the division of work increases as societies increase in volume and density, it is not because of greater variation in the external circumstances, but because the struggle for existence is more severe. [. . .]

The division of labour is, therefore, a result of the struggle for existence, but it is an ameliorated outcome. By virtue of it, opponents are not compelled to fight to a finish, but can co-exist. Also, in proportion to its development, it provides the means of sustenance and survival for a greater number of individuals who would otherwise, in more homogeneous societies, be condemned to extinction. [. . .]

There are several sets of circumstances in which different functions compete. [. . .] In periods of famine or economic crisis, the vital functions have to be maintained at the expense of less essential functions. Luxury industries are ruined, and that part of public resources which had been used to support them is absorbed by food industries, or objects of vital necessity. Or, on the other hand, an organism may reach an abnormal level of activity, out of all proportion to needs, and, in order to meet the expenses of this exaggerated development, it has to deprive others of their share. For example, there are societies with too many civil servants, or too many soldiers, or an excess of officers, intermediaries, or priests, etc. Other occupations suffer as a result of this hypertrophy. But these are all pathological cases. They result from the fact that the organism is irregularly nourished, or because functional equilibrium has been disrupted.

But an objection arises: an industry exists only if it answers a need. A function can only become specialized if this specialization corresponds to some social need. But each new specialization has the result of increasing and improving production. If this advantage is not the reason for the existence of the division of labour, it is its necessary consequence. Thus, an advance only becomes established in a permanent form if individuals feel a need for a greater quantity or quality of products. [. . .] But where could these new demands have come from?

They are produced by the same cause that determines the progress of the division of labour. We have just noted that such progress is due to the increased severity of the struggle. But more severe struggle cannot occur without considerable depletion of forces and ensuing fatigue. But in order for life to be maintained, there must be a replenishment equal to what has been expended. [. . .]

Mental life develops, therefore, at the same time as competition becomes keener, and to the same extent. This progress is seen not just among the élite, but in all social classes. In this respect, it is sufficient to compare the worker with the farm labourer. It is well known that the former is much more intelligent, despite the mechanical nature of the tasks which he often has to perform. Besides, it is not by chance that mental illnesses develop along with civilization, nor that they increase in cities rather than in rural areas, and in large cities more than in small towns. [. . .]

By showing what the division of labour is composed of, this is sufficient to make clear that it could not be otherwise. It entails the sharing out of functions that were previously held in common. But this sharing cannot be performed according to a preconceived plan. It is impossible to know in advance where the demarcation line between tasks will occur when they become divided, for it is not clearly evident in the nature of things, but rather depends on a variety of circumstances. The division of labour, therefore, must proceed in its own way and progressively. Consequently, in such conditions, in order for a function to be divided into two matching, complementary parts, as required by the nature of the division of labour, it is essential for the two specializing parts to be in constant communication throughout the period of dissociation. There is no other way in which one can receive all the functions relinquished by the other, and for their mutual adaptation to occur. But in the same way that an animal colony in which all the members embody a common tissue constitutes a single entity, every aggregate of individuals who are in continuous contact form a society. Therefore, the division of labour can only be produced within a pre-existing society. That is to say, not merely must individuals be materially linked, but it is also necessary for there to be moral links between them. [. . .] It is certainly true that people think everything occurs as a result of freely negotiated private agreements. Thus, it seems as if there is an absence of any social action. But this is to forget that contracts are possible only where there already exists some juridical regulation and, consequently, a society.

Hence, the claim that the division of labour constitutes the fundamental fact of all social life is wrong. [. . .] There is, therefore, a social life external to the whole division of labour, but which is presupposed by the latter. This is exactly what we have established by showing that there are societies whose cohesion is fundamentally due to a community of interests, and it is out of these societies that there have emerged societies in which unity is assured by the division of labour. [. . .]

It is mechanical causes and compelling forces such as blood ties, attachment to the same territory, ancestor worship, a community of shared habits, etc., that bring men together. It is only after the group has been formed on these bases that cooperation becomes organized. [. . .]

If this important fact has been ignored by the Utilitarians, it is because their error derives from the way in which they conceive of the origin of society. They assume that there were originally isolated and independent individuals who, consequently, entered into relationships solely for the purpose of cooperation, because they could have had no other reason to overcome the distance separating them and to enter into association. But this theory, which is so widely held, postulates a veritable *creatio ex nihilio* (creation out of nothing).

SECONDARY FACTORS

The progressively indeterminate common consciousness and its causes

In the first part of this work we observed that the collective consciousness became weaker and vaguer with the development of the division of labour. Indeed, it is through this progressive indetermination that the division of labour emerges as the main source of solidarity. [. . .] In other words, in order for the division of labour to emerge and increase, it is not sufficient for individuals to possess potentialities for special aptitudes, nor that they be persuaded to specialize in these directions, but it is essential that individual variations should be allowed. But they cannot emerge if they are in opposition to some strong and definite state of the collective consciousness, for the stronger this is, the greater the resistance to anything that may weaken it; the more clearly defined it is, the less space it leaves for changes. [. . .]

In a small society, because everyone is obviously placed in the same conditions of existence, the collective environment is essentially concrete. [. . .] But its character changes as societies increase in volume. Because these societies are spread out over a greater area, the common consciousness itself has to transcend all local differences, to dominate more space, and consequently to become more abstract. It is not possible for many general things to be common to all these different environments. [. . .]

It has often been observed that civilization has a tendency to become more rational and more logical. The cause is now obvious. Only that which is universal is rational. It is only the general that is highly regarded. Consequently, the closer the common consciousness is to particular things, the more it is marked by them, the more unintelligible it is. [. . .] But the more general the common consciousness becomes, the more space it allows to individual variations. [. . .] There is nothing fixed except abstract rules, which can be applied freely in quite different ways.

Finally, to the extent that society is extended and concentrated, it absorbs the individual less, and as a result it also cannot restrain the emerging divergent tendencies.

In order to convince ourselves of this it is only necessary to compare large cities with small ones. In the latter, anyone who attempts to break out of established customs encounters often severe resistance. Every attempt at independence is a public scandal, and the general condemnation it attracts is of a kind that discourages imitators. By contrast, in large cities, the individual is much freer of collective bonds.

BOOK III: THE ABNORMAL FORMS
THE ANOMIC DIVISION OF LABOUR

Until now, we have studied the division of labour only as a normal phenomenon. But, like all social facts, and, more generally, like all biological facts, it manifests pathological forms which need to be analysed. Normally, the division of labour produces social solidarity, but it can happen to produce totally different or even opposite results. [. . .]

We shall reduce the exceptional forms of the phenomenon that we are studying to three types. This is not because there cannot be others, but the forms that we are about to discuss are the most general and the most serious.

A first case of this kind is provided for us by industrial or commercial crises, by bankrupticies, which are no less than partial breaks in organic solidarity. [. . .]

The conflict between labour and capital is another, more striking, example of the same phenomenon. As industrial functions become more specialized, the struggle becomes keener rather than solidarity increasing. [. . .]

We shall see in the following chapter that this tension in social relationships is due in part to the fact that the working classes do not really want the conditions imposed upon them, but too often accept them only when constrained and forced to do so, having no means of overcoming them. [. . .]

Nowadays there are no longer any rules which fix the number of economic enterprises, and, in each branch of industry, production is not regulated to remain in line with the level of consumption. We do not wish to draw any practical conclusions from this fact. We do not maintain that restrictive legislation is necessary: this is not the moment to consider its advantages and disadvantages. What is certain is that this lack of regulation is not conducive to the regular harmony of functions. It is true that economists claim that this harmony establishes itself when necessary, thanks to price rises or reductions, which, according to needs, stimulate or slow down production. But, in any case, this harmony is only re-established in this way after breaks in equilibrium and more or less prolonged disturbances have occurred. On the other hand, the more specialized the functions are, the more frequent these disturbances, for, the more complex the organization, the greater the necessity for extensive regulation.

The relationships between capital and labour until now have remained in the same legal state of imprecision. [. . .]

These various examples are therefore varieties of the same species; in all cases, if the division of labour does not produce solidarity, it is because the relationships between the organs are not regulated; they are in a state of *anomie*.

But what gives rise to this state? Since a body of rules is the defined form of relationships that have been established spontaneously and over time between the social functions, one can say *a priori* that the state of *anomie* is impossible wherever solidly linked organs are in sufficient contact for a sufficient length of time.

THE FORCED DIVISION OF LABOUR

But it is not enough that rules exist, for sometimes these very rules are the cause of evil. This is what happens in class wars. The institution of classes or castes constitutes one organization of the division of labour, one that is strictly regulated. Yet it is often a source of dissension. When the lower classes are not, or are no longer satisfied with the role allotted to them through custom or law, they aspire to functions forbidden to them, and try to dispossess those who exercise these functions. From this arise civil wars, which are due to the way in which work is distributed. [. . .]

In order for the division of labour to engender solidarity, it is not, therefore, sufficient that each person has his task: this task must also suit him.

Now, it is this condition which is not met in the example that we are examining. In effect, if the institution of classes or castes sometimes gives rise to painful wrangling, instead of producing solidarity, this is because the distribution of social functions on which the solidarity is based, does not respond, or rather no longer responds to the distribution of natural talents. [. . .]

In short, work is only divided spontaneously if the society is constituted in such a way that social inequalities express exactly the natural inequalities. [. . .]

Contractual relationships necessarily develop with the division of labour, since this division is not possible without exchange, of which the contract is the legal form. In other words, one of the important varieties of organic solidarity is what might be called 'contractual solidarity'. [. . .]

In a given society each object of exchange has, at each moment, a precise value which we could call its social value. This represents the quantity of useful labour which it contains. [. . .]

Having laid down this definition, we shall say that a contract is fully consented to only if the services exchanged have equal social value. [. . .] In order for such equivalence to prevail for contracts, it is necessary that the contracting parties be placed in externally equal conditions. [. . .] If one class in society is obliged to take any price for its services in order to survive, while another can abstain from such action thanks to the resources that it has at its disposal, which are not the result of any social superiority, the second has an unjust legal advantage over the first. In other words, there cannot be rich and poor from birth without there being unjust contracts. [. . .]

CONCLUSION

But if the division of labour produces solidarity, this is not only because it makes each individual an 'exchangist', as the economists say; it is because it creates between men a whole system of rights and duties which bind them together in an enduring way. Just as social similarities give rise to a law and a morality which protect them, so the division of labour gives rise to rules which guarantee peaceful and regular cooperation between the divided functions. [. . .]

But it is not enough that rules exist. They must also be just, and for that to be so, the external conditions for competition must be equal. [. . .]

In a short space of time, profound changes have occurred in the structure of our societies. They have been liberated from the segmentary type with a rapidity and in such proportions that have never before been seen in history. Consequently the morality which corresponds to this social type has regressed, but without another developing fast enough to fill the space left vacant in our consciousness. Our faith has been disturbed: tradition has lost its influence; individual judgement has become emancipated from collective judgement. But, on the other hand, the functions disrupted during the upheaval have not had time to adjust to one another. The new life that emerged so suddenly has not been able to get completely organized, and, most importantly, has not been organized in a way that satisfies the need for justice which has grown stronger in our hearts. If this is the case, the remedy for the evil is not, however, to try to revive traditions and practices which, no longer responding to actual social conditions, can only be revived artificially and in appearance only. We must put a stop to their *anomie*. We must find ways of making these organs function harmoniously, which, at present, clash discordantly. We must introduce greater justice into their relationships by further diminishing the external inequalities which are the source of our ills.

Reading 4

TWO LAWS OF PENAL EVOLUTION

The variations through which punishment (*la peine*) has passed in the course of history are of two kinds: quantitative and qualitative. The laws regarding each kind are, naturally, different.

THE LAW OF QUANTITATIVE VARIATION

It can be formulated as follows: *"The intensity of punishment is greater as societies belong to a less advanced type* (un type moins éléve) *– and as centralised power has more absolute character."*

Let us first explain the meaning of these statements.

There is no great need to define the first. It is relatively easy to recognize whether a social species is more or less advanced than another: one has only to see which is more complex or, if equally complex, which is more organized. Moreover, this hierarchy of social species does not imply that the succession of societies forms a unique and linear series; on the contrary, it is certain that it is better represented as a

Edited and published with permission from: M. Traugott (ed.), *Emile Durkheim on Institutional Analysis,* Chicago, University of Chicago Press, 1977, pp. 153–180. Originally published as 'Deux lois de l'évolution pénale', *L'Année sociologique* **4** (1899–1900), 65–95.

tree with many more or less divergent branches. But on this tree societies are placed higher or lower and are found at a greater or lesser distance from the common trunk. It is only on the condition of considering them in this way that it is possible to speak of a general evolution of societies.

The second factor which we distinguished above should detain us longer. We say of governmental power that it is absolute when it encounters in the other social functions nothing which by its nature balances and efficaciously limits it. In point of fact, a complete absence of all limitation is nowhere to be found; we can even say that it is inconceivable. Tradition and religious belief serve as restraints to even the strongest governments. [. . .]

This observation leads us to another which more directly concerns our subject: the fact *that the more or less absolute character of the government is not an inherent characteristic of any given social type*. If, in effect, it can as easily be found where collective life is extremely simple as where it is extremely complex, it does not belong more exclusively to lower societies than to others. [. . .]

This special form of political organization — givernmental absolutism — does not, therefore, arise from the congenital constitution of the society, but from individual, transistory, and contingent conditions. This is why these two factors of penal evolution — the nature of the social type and that of the governmental organ — must be carefully distinguished. This is because, being independent, they act independently of one another, sometimes even in opposite directions. For example, it happens that in passing from a lower species to other, more advanced types, we do not see punishment decrease, as could be expected, because at the same time the governmental organization neutralizes the effects of social organization. [. . .]

THE LAW OF QUALITATIVE VARIATIONS

The law which we have just established relates exclusively to the magnitude or quantity of punishments. That which we are now about to consider is related to their qualitative modalities. It can be formulated as follows: *Punishments consisting in privation of freedom — and freedom alone — for lengths of time varying according to the gravity of the crime, tend more and more to become the normal type of repression.* Lower societies are almost completely unacquainted with this kind of punishment. [. . .]

On first examination, it doubtless seems quite obvious that, from the day when prisons became useful to societies, men had the idea of constructing them. However, in reality, the existence of prisons assumes that certain conditions, without which they are not possible, have been realized. Prisons imply the existence of public establishments, sufficiently spacious, militarily occupied, arranged in such a way as to prevent communications with the outside, and so on. Such arrangements are not improvised on the spur of the moment; no traces of them exist in less advanced societies. [. . .]

But as the social horizon is extended, as collective life, instead of being dispersed into a vast number of minor foci where it can manage only a meager existence, is concentrated about a more restricted number of points, it simultaneously becomes more intense and more continuous. Because it takes on greater importance, the dwellings of those who are in charge are transformed. They are extended and are organized in view of the more extensive and more permanent functions which are incumbent upon them. The more the authority of those who live in them grows, the more those dwellings are singularized and distinguished from the rest. They take on a grandiose air; they are sheltered by higher walls and deeper moats in such a way as to denote visibly the line of demarcation which thenceforth separates the holders of power and the mass of their subordinates. At that point, the preconditions of the prison come into being. What leads us to suppose that prisons originated in this way is that they often first appeared in the shadow of the king's palace or among the outbuildings of temples and similar institutions. [. . .]

Thus, at the very moment when the establishment of a place of detention became useful in consequence of the progressive disappearance of collective responsibility, edifices which could be used for this purpose were being constructed. Prisons, it is true, were as yet only preventive. But once constituted for this purpose, they quickly took on a repressive nature, at least in part.

EXPLICATION OF THE FIRST LAW

Since the penalty results from the crime and expresses the way in which it affects the public conscience, we must seek the determining cause of the evolution of penal law in the evolution of crime.

Without having to enter into the details of the proofs which justify this distinction, we think that it will be conceded without difficulty that all acts reputed to be criminal by the various known societies can be divided into two fundamental categories: some are directed against collective things (whether ideal or material), of which the principal examples are public authority and its representatives —

mores, traditions, and religion — the others offend only individuals (murders, thefts, violence, and frauds of all kinds). These two forms of criminality are sufficiently distinct to be designated by different words. The first could be called "religious criminality" because attacks against religion are its most essential element and because crimes against traditions or heads of state always have a more or less religious character. We might refer to the second category as "human" or "individual criminality." We also know that crimes of the first type comprise, almost to the exclusion of all others, the penal law of lower societies, but that, on the contrary, they regress to the extent that social evolution proceeds. Meanwhile, attacks against the individual (*la personne humaine*) more and more occupy this entire area. For primitive peoples, crime consists almost solely in not observing the practices of the cult, in violating the ritual taboos, in deviating from the mores of ancestors, in disobeying authority where it is strongly consolidated. On the other hand, for today's European, crime consists essentially in the disruption of some human interest.

Now, these two types of criminality differ profoundly because the collective sentiments which they offend are not of the same nature. As a result, repression cannot be the same for both. [. . .]

If we compare the present with the past, we find that we are not more tolerant of all crimes indiscriminantly, but only of some of them; there are others, on the contrary, toward which we show ourselves to be more severe. However, those for which we evince an ever greater indulgence happen also to be those which provoke the most violent repression. Inversely, those for which we reserve our severity evoke only moderate punishments. Consequently, to the extent that the former cease to be treated as crimes and are withdrawn from penal law to be replaced by the latter, a weakening of the average penalty must necessarily occur. But this weakening can last only as long as does this substitution. A time must come — it has nearly arrived — when the process will have to be completed, when attacks against persons will fill the whole of criminal law, when even what remains of the others will be considered to be dependent on this new form of criminality. The movement of retreat will then stop. There is no reason to believe that human criminality must, in its turn, regress in the same way as the punishments which repress it. Instead, everything leads us to predict that it will develop further, that the list of acts considered criminal will grow longer and that their criminal character will be accentuated. Frauds and injustice which yesterday left the public consciousness indifferent, today arouse its revulsion. And this sensitivity will only become more lively with time. There is not a general tapering off of the entire repressive system; one particular system is giving way but is being replaced by another which, while less violent and less harsh, still has its own severities and is in no way destined to an uninterrupted decline.

Part Three

Sociological Method

Reading 5

THE RULES OF SOCIOLOGICAL METHOD

PREFACE

We are still so accustomed to solving questions according to common-sense notions that we find it difficult to dispense with them in socio-logical discussions. When we believe ourselves to be free of common-sense judgements they take us over unawares. Only long and specialized experience can prevent such failings. We would ask the reader not to forget this. He should always bear in mind that his usual ways of thinking are more likely to be adverse rather than favourable to the scientific study of social phenomena, and he must therefore be wary of his first impressions. [. . .] Our method is in no way revolutionary. It is even, in a sense, essentially conservative, since it considers social facts as things whose nature, however flexible and malleable, is nevertheless not modifiable at will. How much more dangerous is the doctrine which sees these social facts as the mere product of mental combina-tions which a simple dialectical artifice can, in an instant, utterly overthrow.

Similarly, because people are used to depicting social life as the logical development of ideal concepts, a method which makes collec-

From: *Les Règles de la méthode sociologique*, Paris, Alcan, 1895. Translation by Margaret Thompson.

tive evolution dependent on objective conditions that are spatially defined, may be judged as crude and possibly materialist. But we could with more justice claim to be the opposite. In fact, does not the essence of spiritualism lie in the idea that psychological phenomena cannot be directly derived from organic phenomena? Our method is in part merely an application of this principle to social facts. Just as spiritualists separate the realm of the psychological from the biological realm, so shall we separate the psychological from the social; like them, we refuse to explain the more complex in terms of the more simple. Yet, in truth, neither of the labels fits us exactly; the only one we would accept is that of rationalist. Our main objective is to extend the scope of scientific rationalism to human behaviour by showing that, in the light of the past, this behaviour can be reduced to relationships of cause and effect, which a no less rational operation can then transform into rules of action for the future. Our so-called positivism is but a consequence of this rationalism. [. . .]

PREFACE TO THE SECOND EDITION

The proposition that social facts must be treated as things — a proposition which is the very basis of our method — is one of those to have provoked the most argument. It is regarded as paradoxical and scandalous that we should compare the realities of the social world with those of the external world. This was a remarkable misunderstanding of the meaning and significance of this comparison, the intention of which was not to reduce the higher forms of being to lower forms, but, on the contrary, to claim for the former a degree of reality at least equal to that which everyone recognizes in the second. In fact, we do not say that social facts are material things, but that they are things by the same right as material things, though in a different way.

What, in fact, is a thing? A thing differs from an idea in the same way that what we know from the outside differs from what we know from the inside. A thing is any object of knowledge which our understanding does not naturally penetrate; it is everything that we cannot adequately conceptualize by a simple process of mental analysis; it is everything that the mind cannot succeed in understanding except by going outside itself in the form of observations and experiments, which progress from the most external and most immediately accessible characteristics to those which are least visible and most profound. To treat facts of a certain order as things is not, therefore, to classify them in a particular category of reality; it is rather to observe a particular mental attitude towards them. We begin the study of them by adopting the principle that we are totally ignorant of what they are, and that their characteristic properties, like the unknown causes on which they depend, cannot be discovered even by the most careful introspection. [. . .]

Another proposition has been no less vigorously disputed than the previous one: it is the one that states that social phenomena are external to individuals. [. . .]

Social facts do not differ only in quality from psychological facts: they have a different substratum, they do not evolve in the same environment, neither do they depend on the same conditions. This does not mean that they are not also psychological in some sense, since they all consist of ways of thinking or acting. But the states of the collective consciousness are of a different nature from the states of the individual consciousness; they are representations of another kind. The mentality of groups is not the mentality of individuals; it has its own laws. The two sciences are, therefore, as clearly distinct as two sciences can be, whatever relationships there might otherwise be between them.

Nevertheless, there is every reason for making a distinction on this point, which will perhaps throw some light on the argument.

It seems quite clear to us that the substance of social life cannot be explained by purely psychological factors, that is, by the states of the individual consciousness. In fact, what collective representations express is the way in which the group thinks of itself in its relations with objects that affect it. Now the group is constituted differently from the individual and the things which affect it are of another kind. Representations which express neither the same subjects nor the same objects cannot depend on the same causes. To understand the way in which a society conceives of itself and the world that surrounds it, we must consider the nature of the society, not the nature of the individuals. The symbols which represent it change according to what the society is. [. . .]

But once this difference in nature is recognized, one might well ask if individual and collective representations nevertheless ressemble each other, since both are equally representations; and if, as a result of these similarities, certain abstract laws might be common to the two domains. Myths, popular legends, religious conception of all kinds, moral beliefs, etc., express a reality different from individual reality; but it may be that the way in which they attract or repel each other, unite or separate, is independent of their content and is related only to their general quality of being representations. Although they have a different composition, they might behave in their interrelationships as do feelings, images or ideas in the individual. Can we believe, for example, that proximity and similarity, logical contrasts and oppositions, act in the same way regardless of the things they represent? Thus we can begin to imagine the possibility of an entirely formal psychology which would be a sort of common ground for individual psychology and sociology; this is perhaps why certain scholars are reluctant to distinguish too sharply between these two sciences.

Strictly speaking, in the present state of knowledge, the question posed in this way could not be given a categorical solution. In fact, on the one hand, everything that we know about the way in which individual ideas combine together can be reduced to those few, very general and very vague propositions that are commonly called laws of the association of ideas. As for the laws of collective thinking, they are even less well known. Social psychology, whose task it should be to determine these laws, is hardly more than a word which denotes all kinds of varied and imprecise generalities, without any defined object. By comparing mythical themes, popular legends and traditions, and languages, we need to investigate how social representations attract and exclude each other, how they fuse together or remain separate, etc. [. . .]

We need to say a few words about the definition of social facts that we gave in the first chapter. We describe them as consisting of ways of acting or thinking, recognizable by the distinguishing characteristic that they are capable of exercising a coercive influence over individual consciousness. Confusion arose on this subject and should be dealt with. [. . .]

Our definition was found to be both too narrow and, at the same time, too wide, encompassing almost all of reality. It has been said that any physical environment exercises constraint on the beings which are subjected to its action, for, to a certain, extent, they are bound to adapt to it. But between these two modes of coercion there is still the difference separating a physical environment from a moral environment. The pressure exerted by one or several bodies on other bodies or even on other wills should not be confused with the pressure that group consciousness exerts over the consciousness of its members. What is special about social constraint is that it comes, not from the rigidity of certain molecular arrangements, but from the prestige with which certain representations are invested. It is true that habits, whether individual or hereditary, possess in some ways this same property. Habits dominate us, and impose beliefs or practices upon us. But they dominate us from within; for they are wholly within each of us. On the other hand, social beliefs and practices act on us from outside: the influence exerted by them is basically very different from that exerted by habits.

Furthermore, we should not be surprised that other phenomena of nature reveal, in other forms, the very characteristic used to define social phenomena. This similarity comes simply from the fact that both are real things. For everything that is real has a precise nature which compels recognition, must be taken into account and which, even when successfully neutralized, is never completely overcome. And, basically, this is what is most essential about the notion of social constraint: all that it implies is that collective ways of acting or thinking possess a reality outside the individuals who, at any moment in time, conform to it. They are things which have their own existence. The individual encounters them already formed and he can do nothing to eliminate them or to change them; he is obliged to take account of them and it is so much more difficult (though not impossible) for him to change them, since, in varying degrees, they share in the material and moral supremacy that society exercises over its members. Certainly the individual plays a role in their creation. But for a social fact to exist, several individuals, at the very least, must have interacted together, and this joint action must have resulted in a new product. Since this synthesis takes place outside each one of us (since a number of consciousnesses are involved) its necessary effect is to fix, to establish outside ourselves, ways of acting and judging which do not depend on each individual will considered separately. As has been pointed out, there is a word which, provided that one extends its ordinary meaning slightly, expresses rather well this very special manner of existence: the word 'institution'. Without distorting the meaning of this expression, we can, in fact, call all beliefs and all modes of behaviour instituted by the collectivity 'institutions'; sociology can then be defined as the science of institutions, their genesis and their functioning.

WHAT IS A SOCIAL FACT

Before deciding which method is best suited to the study of social facts, it is important to know which are the facts that are termed 'social'.

The question is all the more necessary since this term is used without much precision. It is commonly used to describe nearly all the phenomena which occur within society, even though they may be of little general social interest. But, on this basis, there are, so to speak, no human events which cannot be called social. Every individual drinks, sleeps, eats, and thinks, and it is in society's interest that these functions are exercised regularly. So, if these facts were social ones, sociology would have no subject matter of its own, and its field would be confused with that of biology and psychology.

But in reality there is in every society a specific group of pheno-

mena which are distinguished by characteristics that are quite separate
from those studied by the other natural sciences.

When I undertake my duties as a brother, husband, or citizen and
fulfil the commitments that I have entered into, I perform obligations
which are defined outside myself and my actions, in law and custom.
Even when they conform to my own sentiments and I experience
their reality subjectively, that reality does not cease to be objective;
for it is not I who created these duties; I received them through education. How many times does it happen that we are ignorant of the
details of the obligations which we must assume and that, to know
them, we have to consult the legal code and its authorized interpreters!
Similarly, the believer, from the day he is born, encounters the beliefs
and practices of his religion ready-made; if they existed before him it is
because they exist outside him. The system of signs that I use to express my thoughts, the monetary system that I employ to pay my
debts, the instruments of credit that I utilize in business relationships,
the practices that I follow in my profession, etc., function independently of the use I make of them. If one takes each member of a given
society in turn, the above statements will apply to every one of them.
So, these are ways of acting, thinking and feeling which possess the
remarkable property that they exist outside individual consciousness.

Not only are these types of behaviour and thinking external to
the individual, but they are also endowed with a forceful coercive
power by virtue of which, whether the individual wishes it or not, they
are thrust upon him. Of course, when I conform to them of my own
accord, this coercion is not felt at all, or very little, since it is unnecessary. But it is no less an intrinsic characteristic of these facts, and the
proof is that it asserts itself as soon as I try to resist. If I try to violate
the legal rules, they react against me in such a way as to prevent my
action if there is time, or to nullify it by restoring it to its normal form
if it has already been accomplished but is reparable, or if not reparable
in any other way, by making me pay the penalty for it. But are they
purely moral rules? The public conscience restricts any acts which
offend against it by the surveillance it exercises over the behaviour of
its citizens and the special penalties at its disposal. In other cases the
constraint is less violent, but it does not cease to exist. If I do not
submit to the conventions of society, if my dress takes no account of
the customs observed in my country and class, the laughter I provoke,
and being made a social outcast, produce in a milder form the same
effects as actual punishment. In other cases the constraint is no less
effective, even though indirect. I am not forced to speak French with
my compatriots, nor compelled to use the legal currency, but it is

impossible for me to do otherwise. If I tried to escape this necessity, my attempt would fail miserably. As an industrialist, nothing prevents me from working with processes and methods from the previous century, but if I do so I shall certainly be ruined. So, in fact, even when I can liberate myself from these rules and violate them successfully, it is never without having to fight against them. Even when they are eventually overcome, they make their constraining power sufficiently felt in the resistance present. The enterprises of all innovators, even successful ones, meet opposition of this kind.

Here, then, is a category of facts with very special characteristics: they consist of ways of acting, thinking and feeling that are external to the individual and are endowed with a coercive power by virtue of which they exercise control over him. Consequently, since they consist of representations and actions, they could not be confused with biological phenomena, nor with psychological phenomena which exist only in and through the individual consciousness. Therefore, they constitute a new species of phenomena, and it is to them exclusively that the term 'social' should be given. This term is appropriate for it is clear that, as they do not have the individual as their source of origin, they can have no other substratum then society, either the political society as a whole, or one of the groups that in part compose it, such as religious denominations, political, literary and professional associations, etc. On the other hand, the term 'social' is appropriate only to them, for the word has a distinct meaning only if it designates phenomena not included in any of the already established and classified categories of facts. They are, therefore, the proper field of sociology. It is true that when we define them by the word 'constraint', we risk infuriating those who zealously support absolute individualism. Since they maintain that the individual is completely autonomous, it appears to them that the individual is diminished every time he is made to feel that he is not completely self-determined. But since it is indisputable that most of our ideas and inclinations are not developed by ourselves, but come from outside, they can only become part of us by being imposed upon us. this is all that our definition implies. We know, furthermore, that any social constraint does not necessarily exclude the individual personality.

Yet, since the examples just cited (legal and moral rules, religious dogma, financial systems, etc.) all consist of established beliefs and practices, one might think, as a result of what has been said, that social facts exist only where there are distinct organizations. But there are other facts which, without appearing in these highly crystallized forms, have the same objectivity and the same influence over the individual.

These are what are called 'social currents'. Thus, in a public meeting, the great waves of enthusiasm, indignation and pity that are produced, have as their origin no single individual consciousness. They come to each of us from outside and are likely to sweep us along despite ourselves. Of course, it can happen that by unreservedly abandoning myself to them I do not feel the pressure they exert on me. But it becomes evident as soon as I try to fight against them. If an individual tries to oppose one of these collective manifestations, the sentiments that he is rejecting will turn against him. Now if this external, coercive power asserts itself so clearly in cases of resistance, it is because it exists without our being conscious of it in the cases mentioned above. We are, therefore, victims of an illusion, which makes us believe that we ourselves have produced what was imposed on us from outside. [. . .]

Moreover, to confirm this definition of a social fact, we need only observe a typical experience: the way in which children are brought up. When one looks at the facts as they are and as they have always been, it is immediately obvious that all education consists of a continual effort to impose on the child ways of seeing, feeling and acting which he would not have spontaneously arrived at himself. [. . .] What makes these facts particularly instructive is that the aim of education is precisely to create a social being; one can therefore see that it epitomizes the way in which the social being is historically constituted. [. . .]

Thus, sociological phenomena cannot be characterized by their generality. Thoughts which are found in all individual consciousnesses. or movements repeated by all individuals, are not for that reason social facts. If some people have been satisfied with a definition of them bssed on this characteristic it is because they have confused them with what one might call their individual inclinations. What constitutes social phenomena are the collective beliefs, tendencies and practices of a group. [. . .]

Thus, there are certain currents of opinion which impel us, with varying degrees of intensity according to the time and place, in the direction of marriage, for example, or suicide or towards higher or lower birth rates, etc. These currents are obviously social facts. At first sight they seem inseparable from the forms they assume in particular cases. But statistics provide us with the means of isolating them. They are, in fact, not inaccurately represented by the rates of birth, marriage and suicide, that is, by the figure obtained from dividing the annual average total of births, marriages and suicides by the number of people of an age to marry, have children, or commit suicide. For, since each of these figures includes all individual cases without discrimination, the individual circumstances which may play some part in producing the phenomenon cancel each other out and, consequently, do not enter into its determination. What the average expresses, therefore, is a specific state of the collective mind. [...]

It may be objected that a phenomenon can only be collective if it is common to all members of the society, or at the very least, to a majority, and, therefore, if it is general. This is certainly so, but if it is general it is because it is collective (that is, more or less obligatory), rather than it being collective because it is general. It is a group condition which is repeated in the individuals because it is imposed upon them. It is found in each part because it is in the whole, rather than it being in the whole because it is in the parts. [...]

We thus arrive at the point where we can formulate precisely the field of sociology. It includes only one specific group of phenomena. A social fact is recognized by the power of external coercion which it exercises, or is capable of exercising, over individuals; and the presence of this power is in turn recognizable by the existence of some specific sanction, or by the resistance that it offers to any individual action that would violate it. However, one might also define it by the extent of its diffusion within the group, provided that, as noted earlier, one takes care to add as a second essential characteristic, that it exists independently of the individual forms that it assumes in its diffusion. This last criterion is in certain cases even easier to apply than the previous one. In fact, the constraint is easily observed when it is manifested externally through some direct reaction of society, as in the case of law, morality, beliefs, customs, and even fashions. But when the constraint is merely indirect, such as that exercised through an economic organization, it is not always so discernible. Generality combined with objectivity may, therefore, be easier to establish. Moreover, this second definition is simply another form of the first; for if a way of behaving, which exists outside individual consciousnesses, becomes generalized, it can only do so by imposing itself upon them.

Yet one might wonder if this definition is complete. The facts which have provided the basis for it are all 'ways of doing'; they are of a physiological order. There are also collective 'ways of being', that is, social facts of an anatomical or morphological order. Sociology cannot ignore things which concern the substratum of social life. However, the number and nature of the elementary parts which constitute society, the way in which the parts are distributed, the degree of coalescence they have achieved, the distribution of the population over the land surface, the number and types of means of communication, the form of dwellings, etc., at first sight, do not appear to be related to ways of acting, feeling or thinking.

But, first of all, these various phenomena present the same characteristic that helped us to define the others. These 'ways of being' are imposed on the individual similarly to the 'ways of doing' already mentioned. In fact, when we want to know how a society is divided politically, and how these divisions are composed, and their degree of fusion, we shall not achieve this knowledge by physical inspection and geographical observation; for these divisions are social, even though they have some basis in physical nature. It is only through public law that it is possible to study this organization, for it is law that determines it, just as it determines our domestic and civic relationships. This organization is no less obligatory. If the population crowds into our cities instead of scattering into the countryside, this is because there is a current of opinion, a collective impulse, which imposes this concentration upon individuals. We can no more choose the form of our houses than of our clothes; at least, both are equally obligatory. Channels of communication forcibly determine the direction of internal migrations and commercial exchanges, and even their intensity. Consequently, at the very most, there would be grounds for adding one further category to the phenomena listed as exhibiting the distinctive sign of a social fact, and as this list was not intended to be strictly exhaustive, the addition would not be essential.

But it is not even useful to add to the listing, for these 'ways of being' are but 'ways of doing' that have been consolidated. [. . .] There is thus a whole range of differences of degree, without any break in continuity, spanning the most articulated structural facts and those free currents of social life which have yet to become specifically moulded. They are distinguished only by a degree of consolidation that they exhibit. Both are more or less crystallized forms of life. Certainly, there may be an advantage in reserving the term 'morphological' for social facts which concern the social substratum, but only if we do not forget that they are of the same nature as the others. Our definition will include everything necessary if we say:

> A social fact is every way of acting, whether fixed or not, which is capable of exercising an external constraint on the individual; or, which is general throughout a given society, whilst having an existence of its own, independent of its individual manifestations.

RULES FOR THE OBSERVATION OF SOCIAL FACTS

The first and fundamental rule is to *consider social facts as things*.

At the moment when a new order of phenomena become the

object of a science, they are already represented in the mind, not only through definite images, but also by some sort of crudely formed concepts. Before the first rudiments of physics and chemistry were known, men already had notions about physical and chemical phenomena which went beyond pure perception; such notions, for example, can be found intermingled with all religions. This is because reflection comes before science, which uses it more methodically. Man cannot live among things without developing ideas about them, according to which he regulates his behaviour. But, because these notions are closer to us and more within our grasp than the realities to which they correspond, we naturally tend to substitute them for the realities and even make them the subject of our speculation. Instead of observing, describing and comparing things, we are content to consider our ideas, and to analyse and compare them. Instead of creating a science concerned with realities, we merely carry out an ideological analysis. Certainly this analysis does not necessarily exclude all observation. One can appeal to the facts in order to confirm these notions or the conclusions that are drawn. But the facts intervene only secondarily, as examples or confirmatory proofs: they are not the object of the science, which proceeds from ideas to things, not from things to ideas. [. . .]

If this has been true for the natural sciences, how much more so must it have been true for sociology. Men did not wait for the coming of social sciences in order to develop ideas on law, morality, the family, the state, or society itself, for they needed such ideas in order to live. It is particularly in sociology that these preconceptions, to use Bacon's expression, are in a position to dominate minds and be substituted for things. In fact, social things are actualized only through men; they are a product of human activity. They appear to be nothing more than the implementation of the ideas that we carry within our minds, which may or may not be innate; they are nothing but the application of these ideas to the various circumstances involving relations between people. The organization of the family, of contracts, punishment, the state, and of society, thus appear as simply the embodiment of the ideas that we have about society, the state, justice, etc. Consequently, these facts and others like them seem to have reality only in and through the ideas which produce them and which, therefore, become the subject matter appropriate to sociology. [. . .]

And yet social phenomena are things and should be treated as things. To demonstrate this proposition one does not need to philosophize about their nature, or to discuss the analogies with phenomena of a lower order. It is enough to state that they are the only data available to the sociologist. A thing is, in effect, everything that is given, offered, or rather forced upon, our observation. To treat phenomena as things is to treat them as data which provide the starting point for science. What is given to us are not the ideas that men form about value, for those are inaccesible, but only the actual value at which things are exchanged in the case of economic relations; not some notion or other of the moral ideal, but the sum total of rules which actually determine behaviour; not the idea of utility or wealth, but all the detailed economic organization. It is possible that social life is merely the development of certain notions; but, even supposing this to be the case, these notions are not immediately obvious. They cannot be arrived at directly, but only through the real phenomena which express them. We do not know *a priori* what ideas form the basis of the various currents of social life, nor even if there are any; it is only by going back to their source that we will arrive at knowledge of their origins.

We must, therefore, consider social phenomena in themselves, separate from the conscious beings who represent them; we must study them from the outside as external things, for it is in this guise that they appear to us. If this exteriority proves to be merely apparent, the illusion will be dissipated as science advances, and we shall see the external merging with the internal, so to speak. But this outcome cannot be anticipated and even if social phenomena eventually turn out not to have all the characteristics of things, we must first treat them as if they had. This rule is, therefore, applicable to the whole of social reality, and there is no reason to make any exception. Even phenomena which most seem to consist of arbitrary arrangements must still be considered from this perspective. *The conventional character of a practice or an institution must never be presumed in advance.* If I might be allowed to draw on my own experience, I think I can guarantee that by proceeding in this manner one will often have the satisfaction of seeing the most apparently arbitrary facts revealing, after closer observation, the qualities of consistency and regularity that are symptomatic of their objectivity.

In general, moreover, what was said earlier about the distinctive characteristics of the social fact should be sufficient to reassure us about the nature of this objectivity and to prove that it is not illusory. A thing is principally recognized as such by virtue of the fact that it cannot be modified simply by an act of will. This is not because it is resistant to all modification. But, in order to produce a change, it is not enough to will it: it requires some degree of strenuous effort, owing to the resistance it meets, which cannot always be overcome. We have seen that social facts have this property. Far from being a product of our will, they determine it from outside; it is as if they are moulds into which we are required to cast our actions. Often this requirement is such that we cannot escape it. But even when we manage to triumph over it, the opposition that we meet is sufficient to warn us that we are in the presence of something independent of us. So, in considering social phenomena as things, we shall merely be conforming to their nature.

Finally, the reform needed in sociology is in all respects identical to that which has transformed psychology in the last 30 years. [. . .] scientific psychology arose [. . .] after it had finally been established that states of consciousness can and must be studied externally and not from the perspective of the individual consciousness which experiences them [. . .] This transformation is less difficult to effect in sociology than in psychology. Psychological facts are naturally given as states of the individual, from which they even appear to be inseparable. Internal by definition, it seems as if they cannot be treated as external except by violating their nature. Not only is an effort of abstraction necessary, but also a whole range of procedures and artifices in order to be able to consider them in this way. On the other hand, social facts possess all the characteristics of things in a more natural and immediate way. Law exists in legal codes, daily life is recorded in statistics and historical monuments, fashions are preserved in clothes, and taste in works of art. By virtue of their nature they tend to take form outside individual consciousnesses, since they dominate them. [. . .]

But our predecessors' experience has shown that in order to realize this truth in practice it is not enough to have demonstrated it theoretically or absorbed it internally. The mind has such a natural disposition to fail to recognize it that it is inevitable that we will lapse into past errors unless we submit to a rigorous discipline. We shall formulate the principal rules for this discipline, all of which are corollaries of the previous rule.

(1) The first of these corollaries is: *All preconceptions must be systematically avoided*. [. . .]

(2) But the previous rule is entirely negative. It teaches the sociologist to avoid the dominance of popular notions and to turn his attention towards facts, but it does not say how he must grasp these facts in order to make an objective study of them.

Any scientific investigation is concerned with a specific group of phenomena that fall under the same definition. The first step of the sociologist must therefore be to define the things he is dealing with, so that we know, and he knows, what his subject matter is. This is the first and most necessary condition of any proof and verification; a theory can only be checked if one can recognize the facts of which it provides an account. Furthermore, since this initial definition determines the precise subject matter of science, whether or not this subject matter is a thing will depend on the way in which the definition is formulated.

In order to be objective, the definition must clearly express the phenomena as a function, not of an idea of the mind, but of their inherent properties. [. . .] Hence the following rule: *The subject matter of research should never be anything other than a group of phenomena that have previously been defined according to certain external characteristics, and all phenomena which fit this definition must be included.* [. . .]

However obvious and important this rule is, it is rarely observed in sociology. Precisely because it deals with things that we talk about constantly, such as the family, property, crime, etc., it often appears unnecessary for the sociologist to give a rigorous, preliminary definition. We are so accustomed to using these words, which constantly occur in conversation, that it seems pointless to specify the meaning being given to them. We simply refer to the popular notion of them, but this is often ambiguous. This ambiguity causes us to classify under the same name and with a single explanation things which, in reality, are very different. [. . .] Boundless confusion arises from this. [. . .]

Since the external nature of things is given to us through the senses, we can, therefore, sum up as follows: in order to be objective science must start, not from concepts which are formed independently of the senses, but from sense perceptions. It is from observable data that it must take directly the elements of its initial definitions. [. . .]

(3) But sense experiences can easily be subjective. Hence it is a rule in the natural sciences to discard sense data that are too subjectively dependent on the observer, retaining only those that present a sufficient degree of objectivity. Thus the physicist substitutes for the vague impressions of temperature or electricity the visual representations of the thermometer or the voltmeter. The sociologist must take the same precautions. [. . .] In principle, one might say that social facts are more likely to be objectively represented the more completely separated they are from their individual manifestations. [. . .]

Thus, when the sociologist undertakes the investigation of any order of social facts, he must strive to consider them from an aspect where they appear separate from their individual manifestations. It is because of this principle that we have studied social solidarity, its various forms, and their evolution, through the system of legal rules by means of which they are expressed.

RULES FOR DISTINGUISHING THE NORMAL FROM THE PATHOLOGICAL

Observation carried out according to the preceding rules confuses two types of facts, which in certain respects, are very dissimilar: facts which are as they should be, and facts which ought to be something other than what they are — in other words, normal phenomena and pathological phenomena. We deem it necessary to include them both in the definition with which all research must begin. Although in certain respects they are of the same nature, they do in fact constitute two different varieties which it is important to distinguish. Does science possess the means which allow for this distinction?

The question is of the greatest importance, for on its answer depends one's idea of the role ascribed to science, particularly human science. According to a theory which receives support among the most diverse schools of thought, science cannot teach us anything about what we ought to desire. They say that it recognizes only facts which all have the same value and interest; it observes and explains them, but does not judge them; in science there are none which are blameworthy. Good and evil do not exist in science. It can tell us how causes produce their effects, but not what ends should be pursued. [. . .]

Science is thus devoid, or nearly, of all practical effectiveness, and is therefore without real justification for its existence. For what is the point of working to understand reality, if the knowledge that we acquire cannot serve us in our lives? Can it be said that, by revealing the causes of phenomena, science provides the means to produce them as we choose, and, therefore, to achieve the ends that our will pursues for reasons that go beyond science?. [. . .]

For societies and individual alike, health is good and desirable, and sickness, on the other hand, is bad and should be avoided. So if we find an objective criterion, inherent in the facts themselves, which allows us to distinguish scientifically between health and sickness in the various kinds of social phenomena, science will be in a position to throw light on practical concerns while remaining faithful to its own method. Since at the present time science is not able to affect the individual, it only provides us with general information which becomes appropriately diversified when brought into direct contact with the individual through the senses. The state of health, in so far as science can define it, cannot be applied exactly to any one individual since it can only be established in relation to the most general circumstances, from which everyone deviates to some degree. Nevertheless, it is a valuable reference point for guiding behaviour. [. . .]

All sociological phenomena, like all biological phenomena, are capable of appearing in different forms in different cases, while remaining essentially unchanged. There are two kinds of such forms. The first kind exists generally throughout the species. They are found in most, if not all, individuals. If they are not exactly identical in all the cases observed, but vary from one individual to another, these variations occur within very narrow limits. On the other hand, there are other kinds which are exceptional. Not only are they encountered among a minority, but even where they do occur, they do not usually last for the individual's whole lifetime. They are exceptional both in time and space. We are therefore faced with two distinct varieties of phenomena which must be designated by different terms. The facts which appear in the most general forms we shall call normal and the others we shall call morbid or pathological. If we agree to label as the 'average type' the hypothetical being created by putting together a sort of abstract individuality, the most frequently occurring characteristics in the species with their most frequent forms, we could say that the average and normal types overlap, and that any deviation from this standard of health is a morbid phenomenon. It is true that the average type cannot be distinguished with the same clarity as an individual type, since its constituent attributes are not absolutely fixed but are likely to vary. But the fact that it can be constituted is beyond doubt, since it is the specific subject matter of science, and overlaps with the generic type. The physiologist studies the functions of the average organism, and the sociologist does likewise. Once we know how to distinguish the various social species from each other — and we shall deal later with this question — it is always possible to find the most general form presented by a phenomenon in a particular species.

It can be seen that a fact can be described as pathological only in relation to a given species. The conditions of health and sickness cannot be defined abstractly or absolutely. This rule is not contested in biology. It has never occurred to anyone to think that what is normal for a mollusc should also be normal for a vertebrate. Every species has its own state of health, because it has its own average type, and the health of the lowest species is no less than that of the highest. This same principle applies to sociology though it is often misunderstood. We should abandon this far too prevalent habit of judging an institution, a practice or a moral position as if they were good or bad in or by themselves for all social types indiscriminately.

Since the reference point for judging the state of health or sickness varies according to the species, it can also vary within the same species, if a change is brought about. Thus, from the purely biological point of view, what is normal for the savage is not always so for the civilized person, and vice versa. There is one order of variations above all which it is important to take account of, because they occur regularly in all species: they are variations which relate to age. The health of the old person is not the same as the adult's, and the adult's is not the same as the child's. The same is true for societies. A social fact can therefore only be said to be normal in a particular social species in relation to an equally precise phase of its development. Consequently, to know if it has a right to this label, it is not enough to observe the form it takes in the majority of societies which belong to this species; we must also take care to consider them at the corresponding phase of their evolution. [. . .]

Since the generality which outwardly distinguishes normal phenomena is itself an explicable phenomenon, it would be as well to try to explain it, once it has been directly established by observation. We can have the prior conviction that it is not without cause, but it is better to know exactly what this cause is. The normality of the phenomenon will, in fact, be less open to question if it is demonstrated that the outward sign which had first revealed it is not merely apparent, but is grounded in the nature of things – if, in short, we can establish this factual normality as a normality existing by right. Furthermore, this demonstration will not always consist in showing that the phenomenon is useful to the organism, although this is usually the case, for the reasons just given. But it can also happen, as we remarked, that an arrangement may be normal without being useful, simply because it is necessarily inherent in the nature of the entity. [. . .]

Scientific propositions relating to the normal state will be more immediately applicable to individual cases when accompanied by reasons, for then we shall know better how to recognize those cases where it is appropriate to modify them by their application, and in what way.

There are even circumstances where this verification is absolutely necessary, because the first method, if used in isolation, could bring about an error. This is what happens in periods of transition when the whole species is in process of evolution, without yet being finally stabilized in a new form. In this case the only normal type which is already in effect and grounded in the facts is no longer in touch with the new conditions of existence. [. . .]

So we can formulate the three following rules:

(1) A social fact is normal for a given social type, considered at a given phase of its development, when it occurs in the average society of that species at the corresponding phase of its evolution.

(2) The results of the preceding method can be verified by showing that the general character of the phenomenon is related to the general conditions of collective life in the social type under consideration.

(3) This verification is necessary when this fact relates to a social species which has not yet completed the full course of its evolution. [. . .]

If there is one fact whose pathological nature seems unquestionable, it is crime. All criminologists agree on this point. Though they may explain this pathology in different ways, they are nevertheless unanimous in recognizing it. But the problem needs to be treated less cursorily.

In fact let us apply the prceding rules. Crime is observed not only in the majority of societies of a particular species, but in all societies of all types. There is no society where criminality does not exist. Its form changes, and actions termed criminal are not the same everywhere. But everywhere and always there have been men who have behaved in such a way as to bring upon themselves penal repression. If, at least, as societies pass from lower to higher types, the rate of criminality, that is, the relationship between the annual crime figures and population figures, tended to fall, one might think that crime, while remaining a normal phenomenon, tends to lose this character of normality. But there is no reason to believe that such a regression is real. Many facts would seem rather to demonstrate the existence of a movement in the opposite direction. [. . .]

So we arrive at a conclusion which is apparently rather paradoxical. And let us not deceive ourselves: to classify crime among the phenmena of normal sociology is not merely to say that it is an inevitable though regrettable phenomenon, due to the incorrigible wickedness of men; it is to assert that it is a factor in public health, an integrative part in any healthy society. At first sight, this result is so surprising that it has bothered us for a long time. And yet, once this first impression of surprise has been overcome, it is not difficult to find reasons which explain this normality and, at the same time, confirm it.

First of all, crime is normal because it is completely impossible for a society to be free of it.

As we have shown elsewhere, crime consists of an action which offends certain collective sentiments that are particularly strong and clear-cut. In any given society, to stop actions regarded as criminal from being committed, the sentiments that are offended would have to be found in each individual consciousness without exception, and to the degree of intensity necessary to counteract the opposing sentiments. Even if we suppose that this condition can be effectively achieved, crime would not thereby disappear; it would merely change its form; for the very cause which would thus dry up the sources of criminality would immediately open up new ones. [. . .]

Thus, since there can be no society in which the individuals do not diverge to some extent from the collective type, it is also inevitable that, among these divergences, there are some which appear as criminal in nature. What gives them this nature is not their intrinsic importance, but the importance attributed to these divergences by the common consciousness. If the latter is stronger and has enough authority to make these divergences absolutely minimal, it will also be more sensitive and exacting. By reacting against the slightest deviations with the energy that it otherwise displays only against more serious ones, it will attribute to them the same seriousness. In other words, it will brand them as criminal.

Crime is necessary; it is linked to the fundamental conditions of all social life and, because of that, is useful; for those conditions to which it is bound are themselves indispensable to the normal evolution of morality and law.

Indeed, it is no longer possible today to dispute the fact that not only do law and morality vary from one social type to another, but that they also change within the same type if the conditions of collective existence are modified. But for these transformations to be possible, the collective sentiments which form from the basis of morality have to be open to change, and must therefore be only moderate in intensity. If they were too strong they would no longer be malleable. Any arrangement is, in fact, an obstacle to a new arrangement, and more so when the original arrangement is very strong. The more strongly a structure is articulated, the more resistance it offers to any modification; this is so for functional as well as for anatomical arrangements. If there were no crimes, this condition would not be fulfilled; for such a hypothesis supposes that collective sentiments would have reached a degree of intensity unparalleled in history. Nothing is good indefinitely and without limits. The authority enjoyed by the moral consciousness must not be excessive, otherwise no one would dare attack it, and it would too easily become fixed in an immutable form. For it to evolve, individual originality must be allowed to express itself. [. . .]

This is not all. Apart from this indirect utility, it happens that crime itself plays a useful role in this evolution. Not only does it imply that the way to necessary changes remains open, but that, in certain cases, it directly prepares for these changes. Where crime exists, not only are collective sentiments in the state of malleability necessary to take on a new form, but it often contributes to determining the form that they will take. [. . .]

For socialists, it is capitalist organization, despite its widespread nature, which constitutes a deviation from the normal state, produced by violence and artifice. For Spencer, on the other hand, it is our administrative centralization and the extension of governmental powers which are the radical vices of our societies, in spite of the fact that both progress regularly and universally throughout history. We do not believe that one is ever systematically obliged to decide on the normal or abnormal character of social facts according to their degree of generality. It is always with the help of the dialectic that such questions are settled. [. . .]

The various rules that we have established up to now are therefore closely linked. For sociology to be a true science of things, the generality of phenomena must be taken as the criterion of their normality.

RULES RELATING TO THE CLASSIFICATION OF SOCIAL TYPES

Since a social fact can only be described as normal or abnormal in relation to a given social species, what has been said earlier implies that one branch of sociology is devoted to the constitution and classification of these species. [. . .]

It is not true that science can formulate laws only after reviewing all the facts they express, or form categories only after describing, in their entirety, the individual cases that they include. The true experimental method tends rather to substitute for common facts, demonstrable only when present in large numbers and, consequently, allowing conclusions that are always suspect, 'decisive' or 'crucial' facts, as Bacon said. Such facts have scientific value and interest in themselves and regardless of their number. [. . .]

[A satisfactory method] must, above all, aim to facilitate scientific work by substituting a limited number of types for the indefinite multiplicity of individual cases. But this advantage is lost if these types have been constituted only after a complete investigation and analysis of all the individual cases. It can hardly facilitate the research if it does nothing more than summarize the research that has already been done. It will only be really useful if it allows us to classify characteristics other than those serving as its basis, and if it provides us with frameworks for future facts. Its role is to supply us with points of reference to which we can relate observations other than those which provided these very reference points. For this, the classification must be made, not from a complete inventory of all the individual characteristics, but on the basis of a small number of them, carefully chosen. [. . .] In many cases, even one well carried out observation will be enough, just as one well conducted experiment is often sufficient to establish a law. [. . .]

We know, in fact, that societies are composed of various parts combined together. Since the nature of any resulting combination depends necessarily on the nature and number of the constituent elements and their mode of combination, these characteristics are obviously what we must take as our basis. Indeed we shall see later that it is on them that the general facts of social life depend. Moreover, as they are of a morphological order, we might call that part of sociology whose task is to constitute and classify social types 'social morphology'.

The principle of this classification can be specified even more. We know that these constituent parts of any society are societies of a simpler kind. A people is produced by the bringing together of two or more pre-existing peoples. So if we knew the simplest society that ever existed, to make our classification we would only have to follow the way in which this society compounds itself and how its composites combine together. [. . .]

The term 'simplicity' can only have a precise meaning if it signifies a complete absence of parts. A simple society must therefore be understood to mean any society which does not include others simpler than itself, which at present is not only confined to one single segment, but also shows no trace of any previous segmentation. The 'horde', as we have defined it elsewhere, corresponds exactly to this definition. [. . .]

Once this notion of the horde or the single-segment society has been established — whether it is conceived as a historical reality or as a scientific hypothesis — we have the necessary base for constructing the complete scale of social types. [. . .]

We shall begin by classifying societies according to the degree of organization they manifest, taking as a base the perfectly simple society or the single-segment society. Within these classes different varieties will be distinguished according to whether or not a complete coalescence of the initial segments takes place.

RULES FOR THE EXPLANATION OF SOCIAL FACTS

Most sociologists think they have accounted for phenomena once they have shown what purpose they serve and what role they play. They reason as if phenomena existed only for this role and had no determining cause other than a clear or confused sense of the services they are required to render. [. . .]

But this method confuses two very different questions. Showing how a fact is useful does not explain how it arose nor how it is what it is. The uses which it serves presuppose specific properties which characterize it but do not create them. Our need for things cannot give them a specific nature and, consequently, that need cannot produce them from nothing and endow them with existence.

[. . .]

[A] fact can exist without serving any purpose, either because it has never been adapted to any vital end, or because, having once been useful, it then loses all its usefulness but continues to exist merely by force of habit. There are indeed more instances of such survivals in society than in the human organism. There are even cases where a practice or a social institution changes its functions without thereby changing its nature. [. . .] It is a proposition as true in sociology as biology that the organ is independent of its function, that is, while remaining the same, it can serve different ends. Thus the causes which give rise to its existence are independent of the ends that it serves. [. . .]

Thus, because we allow a place for human needs in sociological explanations we do not revert, even partially, to teleology. For these needs can only influence social evolution if they themselves evolve, and the changes they undergo can only be explained by causes which are in no way predetermined. [. . .]

Therefore when one undertakes to explain a social phenomenon, one must study separately the efficient cause which produces it and the function it fulfils. We use the word 'function' in preference to the word 'end' or 'purpose' precisely because social phenomena generally do not exist for the useful results they produce. What we must determine is whether there is a correspondence between the fact under consideration and the general needs of the social organism, and in what this correspondence consists, without concerning ourselves about whether it was intentional or not. Anyway, all these questions about intention are too subjective to be dealt with scientifically.

Not only must these two kinds of problems be separated, but it is usually appropriate to deal with the first kind before the second. In fact, this order of preference corresponds to the facts. It is natural to seek the cause of a phenomena before trying to determine its effects. This method is all the more logical because once the first question is resolved, it will often help to resolve the second. Indeed, the solid link which joins cause to effect is of a reciprocal character which has not been sufficiently recognized. Undoubtedly, the effect cannot exist without its cause, but the latter, in turn, requires its effect. It is from the cause that the effect derives its energy, but on occasion, it also restores energy to the cause and, consequently, cannot disappear without the cause being affected. For example, the social reaction which constitutes punishment is due to the intensity of the collective sentiments that the crime offends. On the other hand, its useful function is to maintain these sentiments at the same degree of intensity, for they would soon diminish if the offences committed against them went unpunished. [. . .]

If the usefulness of a fact is not the cause of its existence, usually it must be useful in order to be able to survive. [. . .] To explain a vital fact, it is not enough to show the cause on which it depends; we must also — at least in the majority of cases — discover the part that it plays in the establishment of that general order. [. . .]

It is therefore in the nature of society itself that one must look for the explanation of social life. We can understand that, since it infinitely transcends the individual both in time and space, society is in a position to impose upon the individual ways of acting and thinking it has established by its authority. This pressure, which is the distinctive sign of facts, is the pressure that all exert on each individual.

But it will be argued that, since the sole elements that make up society are individuals, the primary origin of sociological phenomena can only be psychological. By reasoning in this way, we can just as easily establish that biological phenomena are explained analytically by inorganic phenomena. Indeed, one can be quite certain that in the living cell there are but molecules of crude matter. But these molecules are connected, and it is these connections which cause the new phenomena that characterize life. It is impossible to find even the germ of this connection in any one of these elements. This is because a whole is not the same as the sum of its parts; it is something different, whose properties differ from those displayed by its constituent parts. [. . .]

By virtue of this principle, society is not the mere sum of individuals, but the system formed by their association represents a specific reality which has its own characteristics. Undoubtedly nothing collective can be produced if there are no individual consciousnesses; this condition is necessary but not sufficient. These consciousnesses must be associated and combined, but combined in a certain way. Social life results from this combination, and it is therefore this combination which explains it. [. . .] In a word, there is the same gap between psychology and sociology as there is between biology and the physical

and chemical sciences. Consequently, every time that a social phenomenon is directly explained by a psychological phenomenon, we may
be sure that the explanation is false.

Perhaps it will be argued that if society, once formed, is, in fact,
the immediate cause of social phenomena, then the causes which have
determined its formation are of a psychological nature. They may agree
that when individuals are in association together, that association can
give rise to a new life, but they claim that this can only happen for
individual reasons. But, in reality, as far back as one can go in history,
the act of association is the most obligatory of all, because it is the
source of all other obligations. By reason of my birth, I am obliged to
associate with given people. It may be said that later, when I am an adult,
I acquiesce in this obligation by the very fact that I continue to live
in my country. But what does it matter? This acquiescence does not
take away its imperative character. Pressure accepted and undergone
with good grace does not cease to be pressure. What can be the meaning
of such acquiescence? Firstly, it is forced, for in the vast majority of
cases it is physically and morally impossible for us to shed our nationality; such a change is even taken to be apostasy. Next, it cannot relate
to the past, to which I was unable to consent, but which, nevertheless,
determines the present: I did not choose the education that I received,
but it is my education, more than any other cause which roots me to
my native soil. Finally, this acquiescence can have no moral value for
the future, since this is unknown. I do not even know all the duties
which might fall to me one day in my capacity as a citizen. How could
I acquiesce in them in advance? We have shown, then, that everything
that is obligatory has its origins outside the individual. [. . .]

Collective representations, emotions and tendencies are generated
not by certain states of individual consciousnesses, but by the conditions under which the social body as a whole exists. [. . .]

Hence we arrive at the following rule: *The determining cause of a
social fact must be sought among antecedent social facts, and not
among the states of the individual consciousness.* Moreover, it can easily
be seen that everything that has already been said applies both to determining the function as well as the cause. The function of a social fact
can only be social, that is, it consists of the production of socially
useful effects. Certainly it can and does happen that, as a consequence,
it also serves the individual. But this fortunate result is not the immediate rationale for its existence. We can therefore complete the preceding
proposition by saying: *The function of a social fact must always be
sought in its relationship to some social end.* [. . .]

The primary origin of any social process of any importance must be sought in the internal constitution of the social environment. [. . .]

The main effort of the sociologist must therefore be directed towards discovering the different properties of that environment which are likely to influence the course of the social phenomena. Up to now, we have found two sets of characteristics which eminently satisfy this condition; these are, firstly, the number of social units or, as we have also called it, the 'volume' of the society; and, secondly, the degree of concentration of the mass, or what we have called the 'dynamic density'. [. . .]

We have shown elsewhere how any increase in the volume and dynamic density of societies profoundly modifies the basic conditions of collective existence, by making social life more intense, and by extending the horizon of thought and action of each individual. [. . .]

But the kind of preponderance that we attribute to the social environment and, more especially, to the human environment does not imply that we must see it as a sort of ultimate, absolute fact beyond which there is no point in going further. On the contrary, it is obvious that its state at any moment in history is itself dependent on social causes, some of which are inherent in the society itself, whilst others are related to the interactions between the society and its neighbours. Furthermore, science knows no primary causes, in the absolute sense of the word. For science, a fact is primary simply when it is general enough to explain a great number of other facts. The social environment is certainly a factor of this type, for the changes which are brought about within it, whatever the causes may be, have repercussions in all directions of the social organism and cannot fail to affect all its functions in some degree. [. . .]

The successive stages through which humanity passes do not engender each other [. . .] We would need to concede that there is an inherent tendency which constantly impels humanity to go beyond the results already achieved, either to realize itself fully, or to increase its happiness, and the object of sociology would be to rediscover the way in which this tendency developed. [. . .] Thus all that we can arrive at experimentally in the species, is a series of changes between which there is no causal link. The antecedent state does not produce the subsequent one, but the relationship between them is exclusively chronological. In these conditions, all scientific prediction is impossible. We can certainly say how things have succeeded one another up to the present, but not in what order they will succeed one another in the future, because the cause on which they are supposed to depend is not scientifically determined or determinable. [. . .]

RULES RELATING TO THE ESTABLISHMENT OF PROOFS

We have seen that sociological explanation consists exclusively in establishing relationships of causality, that it is to do with connecting phenomena to their causes, or, on the contrary, causes to their useful effects. Since social phenomena clearly escape the experimenter's control, the comparative method is the only appropriate one for sociology. [. . .]

If therefore we wish to use the comparative method scientifically, that is, in conformity with the principle of causality as it arises from science itself, we must take the following proposition as the basis of the comparisons that we make: *The same cause always corresponds to the same effect.* Thus, to return to the examples quoted earlier, if suicide depends on more than one cause, this is because, in reality, there are several types of suicide. The same is true of crime. For punishment, on the other hand, if we believed that it could be explained equally well by different causes, this is because we did not see the common element found in all antecedents, by virtue of which they produce their common effect.

In any case, if the various procedures of the comparative method are applicable to sociology, they do not all possess equal powers of proof. The so-called method of 'residues', in so far as it does constitute a form of experimental reasoning, is of no use in the study of social phenomena. Apart from the fact that it can only be useful in the fairly advanced sciences, since it presupposes that a large number of laws are already known, social phenomena are much too complex to be able, in a given case, to eliminate the effect of all causes except one.

For the same reason both the method of agreement and the method of difference are not easily usable. They suppose that the cases compared either agree or differ on one single point. [. . .]

But for the method of concomitant variations it is quite different. Indeed, for this method to be used as proof, it is not necessary to exclude rigorously all the variations that differ from those we are comparing. The mere parallelism in values through which the two phenomena pass, provided that it has been established in an adequate number of sufficiently varied cases, is the proof that a relationship exists between them. This method owes its validity to the fact that it arrives at the causal relationship, not from outside, as in the preceding methods, but from within. It does not simply show us two facts which either accompany or exclude each other externally, so that nothing proves directly that they are joined by an internal bond. On the contrary, the method shows them interacting with each other in a continuous way, at least with regard to their quantity. This interaction, in itself, is sufficient to demonstrate that they are no strangers to each other. [. . .]

It is true that the laws established by this procedure do not always appear directly in the form of causal relationships. The concomitance may be due to the fact, not that one of the phenomena is the cause of the other, but that they are both the effects of the same cause, or, again, that there exists between them a third phenomenon, which is interposed and unnoticed, and is the effect of the first and the cause of the second. The results to which this method leads therefore need to be interpreted. [. . .] For example, it can be established quite definitely that the tendency towards suicide varies according to education. But it is impossible to understand how education can lead to suicide; such an explanation contradicts the laws of psychology. Education, particularly when confined to elementary knowledge, reaches only the most superficial regions of consciousness, whereas the instinct for preservation is one of our basic tendencies. It could not therefore be significantly affected by a phenomenon of such remote and weak influence. We thus begin to wonder if both facts might not be the consequence of a single state. This common cause is the weakening of religious traditionalism which strengthens both the need for knowledge and the tendency towards suicide. [. . .]

But we must not believe that sociology is significantly inferior to the other sciences because it can scarcely use more than one experimental procedure. This disadvantage is, in fact, compensated by the wealth of variations which are available for the sociologist's comparisons, riches without example in other realms of nature. [. . .] Social life, by contrast, is an uninterrupted series of transformations, parallel to other transformations in the conditions of collective existence. We have at our disposal information concerning transformations not only in recent times, but also a great number of transformations through which extinct peoples have passed. Despite gaps, the history of humanity is in other ways as clear and complete as the history of animal species. Furthermore, there is a multitude of social phenomena which occur throughout society, but which assume diverse forms according to regions, occupations, religious faiths, etc. Such are, for example, crime, suicide, birth, marriage, savings, etc. [. . .]

Comparative sociology is not a special branch of sociology; it is sociology itself in so far as it ceases to be purely descriptive and aspires to account for facts.

Part Four

Suicide

Reading 6
SUICIDE

PREFACE

Instead of taking pleasure in metaphysical meditation on social themes, the sociologist should take as the object of his research groups of clearly circumscribed facts, which are capable of ready definition and have recognizable limits, and he must adhere strictly to them. [. . .]

We have chosen suicide for this particular study from among many different subjects that we have had occasion to study during the course of our teaching because it seemed to be a particularly opportune example, and one which is unusually easily defined. Even so, some preliminary work has been necessary to outline it. On the other hand, in compensation, when one focuses in this way, one succeeds in finding real laws that demonstrate the possibilities of sociology much better than any dialectical argument. We shall be examining the laws that we hope to have established. We are quite likely to have made a few mistakes or to have made inductions beyond the observable facts. But at least each proposition is accompanied by proofs, which we have tried to make as plentiful as possible. Above all, we have tried hard to separate the arguments and the interpretations from the facts in each case. [. . .]

Edited and translated from: *Le Suicide: étude de sociologie*, Paris, Alcan, 1897. Translation by Margaret Thompson.

Sociological method as we practise it is entirely based on the fundamental principle that social facts must be studied as things; that is, as realities external to the individual. No precept has been more challenged, but none is more fundamental. For sociology to be possible it must first have an object, and one which is exclusive to sociology. It must take cognizance of a reality which does not belong to other sciences. But if there is ·nothing real beyond individual consciousness then sociology must disappear for lack of any subject of its own. The only objects to which this observation might be applied are mental states of the individual, since nothing else exists. However, that is the field of psychology. In fact, from this point of view, everything of significance, for example concerning marriage, the family, or religion, consists of individual needs to which these institutions are simply a response — paternal love, filial love, sexual desire, what used to be called religious instinct, etc. The institutions themselves, with their diverse and complex historical forms, become negligible and of little significance. [. . .]

But it seems hardly possible to us, on the contrary, that there will not emerge from every page of this book, evidence that the individual is dominated by a moral reality which transcends him — collective reality. When one sees that each population has its own suicide rate and that this rate is more constant than the general mortality, and that, if it changes, it does so according to a coefficient of growth specific to that society; when it seems that variations according to different times of the day, month and year merely reflect the rhythm of social life; and when one observes that marriage, divorce, family, religious society, the army, etc., affect it according to definite laws, some of which can even be expressed in numerical form, one stops seeing these states and institutions as just inconsequential, ineffective ideological arrangements. Rather, they are felt to be real, living, active forces, which, because of the way in which they determine the individual, adequately demonstrate that they do not depend on him; even if the individual enters as an element in the emerging combination, to the extent that these forces become formed, they are imposed upon him. In these circumstances it becomes clear that sociology can and must be objective, since it confronts realities which are as definite and substantial as the realities that concern the psychologist or biologist.

INTRODUCTION

Since the word suicide keeps occurring in the course of this discussion, it might seem as if everyone knows its meaning, and that definition is superfluous. But, in reality, words in everyday language, like the concepts they express, are always ambiguous, and the scholar who uses them in their usual sense, without submitting them to further definition, risks serious confusion. [. . .]

The first task, therefore, must be to determine the order of facts that we intend to study under the label of suicide. Accordingly, we shall inquire whether, among the different kinds of death, there are some which have common characteristics that are objective enough to be recognized by any honest observer, specific enough not to be found elsewhere, but, at the same time, sufficiently similar to those generally called suicides so that we can keep the same expression without distorting the usual meaning. If such are found, we can group together under this label all the facts which show these distinctive charactersistics, regardless of whether the class thus formed fails to include all cases labelled in this way or, inversely, includes some which are normally classified otherwise. What is important is not simply to express more precisely what the average person understands by the term suicide, but to establish a category of objects which can be usefully classified in this way and have an objective basis, corresponding to a definite order of things. [. . .]

So we come to the first formula: the term suicide is applied to any death which results directly or indirectly from a positive or negative act carried out by the victim himself.

But this definition is incomplete; it fails to distinguish between two very different sorts of deaths. The same classification and treatment cannot be given to the death of a person in a hallucinatory state who throws himself from a high window, believing it to be at street level, and to the death of a sane person who takes his life knowing what he is doing. In one sense there are a few deaths that are not the direct or indirect consequence of some steps taken by the person concerned. The causes of death are more often external than internal and they affect us only if we venture into their sphere of action.

Shall it be said that suicide exists only if the act resulting in death was carried out by the victim with this result in mind? That only he who wished to kill himself really kills himself and that suicide is intentional homicide of oneself? In the first place, this would be defining suicide by a characteristic which, whatever its interest and importance might be, would at least suffer from not being easily recognizable because it is not easy to observe. How do we know what the agent's motive was and whether, when he took his decision, it was in fact death that he desired or whether he had some other aim? Intention is too intimate a thing to be understood from outside other than by gross approximation. It even escapes self-observation. How often do we mistake the real reasons for our actions? We are constantly explaining actions deriving from petty feelings or blind routine as being due to noble passions or lofty considerations.

Besides, in general, an act cannot be defined by the ends that the actor is pursuing, for an identical pattern of behaviour can be adapted to many different ends without changing its nature. And indeed, if suicide existed only when the intention to kill oneself was present, then the term suicide could not be used for facts which, despite apparent differences, are basically identical to those generally called suicide and which cannot be called by any other name without rendering the term useless. The soldier who goes out in front to face certain death to save his regiment does not want to die, and yet he is not the author of his own death in the same way as the industrialist or merchant who kills himself to avoid the shame of bankruptcy? The same can be said of the martyr who dies for his faith, the mother who sacrifices herself for her child, etc. Whether the death is simply accepted as a regrettable but inevitable condition given the purpose, or whether it is expressly desired and sought for its own sake, in both cases the person renounces his existence, and the different ways of doing so can be only varieties of a single class. They possess too many fundamental similarities not to be combined in the same generic expression, though subsequent distinctions of types within this established genus are necessary. Certainly, in popular usage, suicide is first and foremost the act of despair of the man who does not wish to live. But, in fact, though one is still attached to life at the moment of leaving it, it is abandoned none the less; and there are clearly essential characteristics common to all acts in which a living person gives up what must be his most precious possession. On the other hand, the diversity of motives which might have prompted these decisions can give rise to only secondary differences. So when devotion goes as far as the definite sacrifice of life, it is, scientifically speaking, a suicide; we shall see later of what sort it is. .

What is common to all possible forms of this supreme renunciation is that the determining act is carried out in full knowledge; the victim, at the moment of acting, knows what must be the result of his action, whatever the reason that led him to act in that way. All deaths which have this particular characteristic are clearly distinct from all others where the victim is either not the agent of his own death, or is its unconscious agent. They differ by an easily recognizable characteristic, for it is not an insoluble problem to discern whether or not the individual knew in advance the natural consequences of his action. Therefore, they form a definite, homogeneous group, distinguishable from any other, and consequently they must be designated by a special term. The term suicide is appropriate and there is no reason to create another, for the vast majority of deaths that are so designated are in fact part of this group. We can say conclusively, therefore, that: *suicide is applied to every case of death which results directly or indirectly from a positive or negative act, carried out by the victim himself, knowing that it will produce this result.* An attempt is an act defined in the same way, but falling short of actual death. [. . .]

But if the act is defined this way, is it of interest to the sociologist? Since suicide is an individual act which affects only the individual, and would seem to depend exclusively on individual factors it must therefore belong to the field of psychology. Surely one ordinarily explains the suicide's decision in terms of his temperament, character, and biographical events?

At this point it is not necessary to consider to what extent and under what conditions it is legitimate to study suicides in this way, but there is no doubt that they can be viewed in an entirely different light. If, instead of seeing suicides only as isolated, individual events that need to be examined separately, one considers all suicides committed in a particular society during a specific time period as a whole, it is evident that the total thus obtained is not simply a sum of independent units, a collective total, but constitutes in itself a new fact *sui generis*, which has its own unity and individuality, and therefore, its own pre-eminently social nature. In fact, for a particular society, provided that the observation is not carried out over too long a period, the statistics are almost invariable. [. . .] This is because the circumstances of life of whole populations remain essentially the same from year to year. Sometimes there are greater variations; but they are somewhat exceptional. They are always contemporaneous with some crisis which temporarily affects the social state. [. . .]

At every moment of its history each society has a certain tendency towards suicide. The relative intensity of this tendency is measured by taking the relationship between the total of voluntary deaths and the population of all ages and sexes. We shall call this numerical datum *the rate of mortality due to suicide, characteristic of the society under consideration.* It is generally calculated in proportion to a million or a hundred thousand inhabitants. [. . .]

The suicide rate therefore constitutes an order of facts which is unified and definite, as is shown by both its permanence and its variability. The permanence would be inexplicable if it was not related to a group of distinctive characteristics, united with each other, which assert themselves simultaneously despite the diversity of accompanying circumstances; and the variability testifies to the individual and concrete nature of these same characteristics, since they vary with the individual character of society itself. In short, these statistical data expresses the tendency to suicide with which each society is collectively afflicted. We will not say at this point what this tendency consists of, whether it is a *sui generis* state of the collective mind, with its own reality, or wheather it represents only the sum of individual states. Although the preceding considerations are difficult to reconcile with this latter hypothesis, we reserve this problem for treatment later in the course of this work. Whatever one's opinion on this matter, such a tendency certainly exists in one form or another. Every society is predisposed to produce a certain number of voluntary deaths. This predisposition can therefore be the object of a special study which belongs to sociology. This is the study we are about to undertake.

Our intention is not to compile an exhaustive inventory of all the conditions that give rise to individual suicides, but simply to examine those on which the definite fact that we have called the social suicide rate depends. These two questions are very distinct, even though they may be related. In fact, there are certainly many individual conditions which are not sufficiently general to affect the relationship between the total number of voluntary deaths and the population. They may perhaps cause this or that individual to kill himself, but not cause the society as a whole to have a greater or lesser tendency towards suicide. Since they are not related to a certain condition of social organization, they have no social consequences. They are, therefore, of interest to the psychologist, but not the sociologist. The sociologist studies causes which affect not the isolated individual but the group. Therefore, among the factors of suicide, the only ones which concern him are those which affect society as a whole. The suicide rate is the product of these factors. This is why we must confine our attention to them. [. . .]

HOW TO DETERMINE SOCIAL CAUSES AND SOCIAL TYPES

The results of the preceding section are not entirely negative. We have in fact established that for each social group there exists a specific tendency towards suicide, which is explained neither by the organic-psychological constitution of individual nor by the nature of the physical environment. Therefore, through a process of elimination, it must necessarily depend on social causes and be in itself a collective phenomenon; certain facts that we have examined, particularly geographical and seasonal variations in suicide, have led us directly to this conclusion. [. . .]

Unfortunately, classification of suicides of sane persons according to their morphological forms or characteristics is impracticable because there is a total lack of the necessary documentation. To be viable it would need good descriptions of many individual cases. One would need to know the suicide's psychological state at the moment of his decision, how he prepared to carry it out, how it was finally executed, whether he was agitated or depressed, calm or excited, anxious or irritated, etc. [. . .]

But we can achieve our end by another method, by reversing the order of study. In effect, there can be only as many different types of suicide as there are different causes. For each type to have its own nature, it must also have special conditions of existence. The same antecedent or group of antecedents cannot sometimes produce one result and sometimes another, otherwise the difference between the second and the first would itself be without cause, which would deny the principle of causality. Any specific difference observed in the causes, therefore, implies a similar difference between the effects. Consequently we can determine the social types of suicide by classifying the causes which produce them, rather than by classifying them directly according to their previously described characteristics. Without seeking to know why they are different from each other, we shall first study the social conditions which are responsible for them; then we shall group these conditions according to their similarities and differences into a certain number of separate classes, and we can be sure that a specific type of suicide will correspond to each of these classes. In a word, instead of being morphological, our classification will be aetiological from the start. [. . .] Thus we shall proceed from causes to effects and our aetiological classification will be complemented by a morphological classification, which will serve to verify the former, and vice versa.

In all respects, this reverse method is the only one suitable for the special problem that we have raised. We must not forget that it is the social suicide rate that we are studying. The only types of interest to us, therefore, are those which contribute to its formation and bring about its variations. It has not been established that all individual sorts of voluntary death have this property. There are some which, though general to a certain degree, are not linked or not sufficiently linked to the moral character of society to enter as a characteristic element into the special physiognomy of each people in relation to suicide. [. . .]

But how do we get at the causes?

In the legal statements which are made every time a suicide is committed, a note is made of the motive (family troubles, physical or other pain, guilt, drunkenness, etc.) which seems to have been the determining cause, and in the statistical records of almost every country there is a special table containing the results of these enquiries under the title: 'Presumed motives for suicides'. It would seem natural to take advantage of this work that has already been done and to begin our research by comparing these documents. They appear to show the immediate antecedents of different suicides; it would seem to be a good method for understanding the phenomenon that we are studying to return firstly to the most immediate causes, and then to proceed to other more distant causes in the series of phenomena, if it seems necessary.

But, as Wagner commented long ago, what are taken to be statistics about suicide motives are in reality statistics about the opinions concerning such motives as held by officials, often minor ones, responsible for providing such statistical information. Unfortunately, as we are aware, official statements are often very faulty even when they refer to obvious material facts that are comprehensible to any conscientious observer and require nothing in the way of evaluation. How much more suspect must they be considered to be when they attempt not simply to record a completed act but to interpret and explain it! It is always a difficult problem to specify the cause of a phenomenon. The scholar requires all sorts of observations and experiments to resolve just one of these questions. Human volition is the most complex of all phenomena. Consequently one must question the worth of these improvised judgements which, based on some hastily collected bits of information, claim to assign a specific origin to each individual case. As soon as some of the facts commonly believed to lead to despair are thought to have been discovered in the victim's past then further search is considered useless and, if the victim is supposed to have recently lost money, experienced family problems, or indulged a taste for alcohol, responsibility is assigned to his drunkenness, domestic unhappiness, or financial loss. Such suspect data cannot be taken as the basis of an explanation for suicide.

Furthermore, even if such data had more credibility, they would not be very useful, because the motives attributed to suicides, whether right or wrong, are not their true causes. The proof of this is that the proportion of cases attributed by the statistics to each of these presumed reasons remains almost identically the same, whereas the absolute numbers, on the contrary, show extreme variations. In France, from 1856 to 1878, suicides rose about 40%, and by more than 100% in Saxony during the period 1854–1880 (1,171 cases instead of 547). Yet in both these countries each category of motives retains the same relative importance from one period to the next.

If one considers that the figures reported here are, and can only be, gross approximations, and that, consequently, too much importance should not be attached to small differences, it can be seen that they remain effectively constant. But for the contributory share of each presumed reason to have remained proportionally the same while suicide is twice as prevalent, would require us to accept that each has doubled its effect. It cannot be fortuitous that they all became twice as fatal at the same time. We are forced to conclude that they all depend on a more general state, which they all more or less faithfully reflect. This is what makes them to varying degrees productive of suicide and, consequently, is its true determining cause. It is this state that we must study, without wasting time on any distant repercussions that it might have on the consciousness of individuals. [. . .]

The reasons ascribed for suicide, or the reasons which the suicide gives for his act, are often only apparent causes. Not only are the reasons merely individual repercussions of a general state, they also express this state very unfaithfully, since they remain the same whilst it does not. It might be said that they reveal the individual's weak points, through which the external current bringing pressure for self-destruction finds its easiest point of entry. But they are not part of this current itself, and therefore they cannot help us to understand it.

So we are not sorry that certain countries like England and Austria have stopped collecting these supposed causes of suicide. Statistical efforts should be given a different direction. Instead of trying to solve these insoluble problems of moral casuistry, they should be concerned with noting more carefully the social concomitants of suicide. In any case, we are making it a rule not to introduce into our research any data that are suspect or not very informative; in fact specialists in suicide have never succeeded in producing any interesting laws from such data. We shall therefore refer to them only occasionally when they seem to be particularly significant and to offer special guarantees. We shall proceed immediately to seek to determine the causes leading to suicide without concerning ourselves with the forms they may assume in individual cases. In order to achieve this we will leave to one side the individual, with his motives and ideas, and examine the different social environments (religious beliefs, family, political society, occupational groups, etc.) as a function of which variations in suicide occur. Only then shall we return to the individual to study how these general causes become individualized to produce the resulting homicidal effects. [. . .]

EGOISTIC SUICIDE

First we will consider the ways in which different religious denominations affect suicide.

A brief glance at a map of suicide in Europe makes it clear immediately that in the really Catholic countries such as Spain, Portugal and Italy, suicide has not developed very much, whilst in Protestant countries like Prussia, Saxony and Denmark, it is at its maximum. [. . .] Obviously these are not all on the same level intellectually and morally; but the similarities are sufficiently marked to enable us to attribute to denominational differences the evident contrast that they present with respect to suicide.

However, this first comparison is still too summary. Despite the existence of some similarities, the populations of these different countries do not have identical social environments. The civilizations of Spain and Portugal are much lower than that of Germany and this inferiority could conceivably be the reason for the lower level of suicide that we have noted. In order to avoid this source of error and to establish more definitely the influence of Catholicism and Protestantism on the tendency to suicide, the two religions need to be compared in the context of a single society.

Among the major German states, Bavaria has by far the fewest suicides. There have been scarcely 90 per million inhabitants each year since 1874, while Prussia has 133 (1871–75), the duchy of Baden 156, Wurtemberg 162, Saxony 300. And Bavaria also has the most Catholics: 713.2 to 1,000 inhabitants. On the other hand, comparison of the different Bavarian provinces shows suicides to vary in direct proportion to the number of Protestants and in inverse proportion to that of Catholics. [. . .]

Switzerland provides us with an interesting case from the same point of view. Because German and French populations co-exist there, it is possible to observe separately the influence of religious denominations on each race. In fact, its influence is the same on both. Catholic cantons are shown to have four or five times fewer suicides than Protestant cantons, whatever the nationality. [. . .]

Thus, everywhere without exception, Protestants evidence many more suicides than members of other denominations.

The propensity of Jews to commit suicide is always less than that of Protestants; in general terms, though to a lesser degree, it is also lower than that of Catholics. Occasionally, however, this latter relationship is reversed, particularly in the recent period. [. . .] It is still very rare for them to exceed the Catholic rate. Furthermore, it has to be remembered that Jews live more exclusively in cities and work in intellectual occupations more than members of other denominations. For this reason they have a greater inclination to commit suicide than adherents of other denominations, owing to reasons other than religion. Therefore, if the Jewish rate is so low, despite this aggravating circumstance, it must be assumed that this religion has the fewest suicides of all, other things being equal.

Having established these facts, how are they to be explained?

Bearing in mind that Jews tend to be in a small minority everywhere, and that in most of the societies where the previous observations were made Catholics were in a minority, it is tempting to find in these facts the cause that explains the relative rarity of voluntary deaths in these two denominations. Clearly, where minority denominations face the hostility of surrounding populations they are obliged to exercise strict control and very rigorous discipline over themselves in order to exist. [. . .]

But, firstly, suicide is insufficiently an object of public condemnation for the small amount of blame it incurs to have such an influence, even for those minorities which have to pay special attention to public opinion because of their situation. [. . .] Anyway, this explanation would not account for the respective situations of Protestants and Catholics [. . .] whatever the proportional distribution of these two denominations in the population, wherever it has been possible to compare them with regard to suicide, Protestants are found to kill themselves much more frequently than Catholics. [. . .] Therefore, even if the great difference between the two religions was partly caused by the need for minorities to exercise prudence, the largest share is certainly due to other causes.

We shall discover these other causes in the character of the two religious systems. Nevertheless, they both prohibit suicide with equal strength; not only do they morally condemn it with great severity, but also they both teach that a new life begins beyond the grave where men are punished for their evil deeds, and suicide is regarded as one of these just as much by Protestantism as by Catholicism. Finally, in both religions these prohibitions are regarded as being of divine origin; they are not represented as the logical conclusion of correct reasoning, but their authority is found in God himself. Thus, if Protestantism is less conducive to the development of suicide, it is not due to a different attitude to that of Catholicism. Therefore, since both religions have the same teaching on this particular subject, the different effect that they have on suicide must derive from one of the more general differentiating characteristics.

The only fundamental difference between Catholicism and Protestantism is that the latter allows free inquiry to a much greater extent than the former. [. . .]

The first conclusion that we reach, therefore, is that the propensity for suicide of Protestantism must relate to the spirit of free inquiry that characterizes this religion. This relationship needs to be properly understood. Free inquiry itself is merely the effect of another cause. [. . .] the overthrow of traditional beliefs. [. . .]

So if Protestantism allows more freedom to individual thought than Catholocism, it is because it has fewer common beliefs and practices. Now, a religious society cannot exist without a collective creed and the more extensive the creed the more unified and strong is the society. [. . .] Thus we arrive at the conclusion that the superiority of Protestantism with respect to suicide results from it being a less strongly integrated church than the Catholic church.

This also explains the case of Judaism. In fact, the criticism to which Jews have for long been subjected to by Christianity has given rise to feelings of exceptional solidarity among them. [. . .] Furthermore, the ostracism to which they are subjected is only one of the causes leading to this result; the very character of Jewish beliefs must make a large contribution to it. Like all early religions, in reality Judaism fundamentally consists of a set of practices that minutely govern all details of life and leave little latitude to individual judgement. [. . .]

Two important conclusions emerge from this chapter.

First, we see why in general suicide increases with knowledge. But knowledge does not determine this increase. It is innocent in this respect and it would be totally unjust to accuse it; the example of the Jews demonstrates this point. But these two facts are simultaneous products of a single general condition which appears in different forms. Man seeks knowledge and he kills himself because the religious society of which he forms part has lost its cohesion; but he does not kill himself because of his knowledge. It is not the learning that he acquires which disorganizes religion; but because religion becomes disorganized, his need for learning is awakened. [. . .]

If religion protects man against the desire to kill himself, it is not because it preaches respect for his person based on arguments *sui generis*, but because it is a society. What constitutes this society is the existence of a certain number of beliefs and practices common to all the faithful which are traditional and-therefore obligatory. The more numerous and strong these collective states are, the more strongly integrated is the religious community, and the greater its preservative value. The particular details of the dogmas and rites are secondary. The

essential thing is that they are capable of supporting a sufficiently intense collective life. Because the Protestant church does not have the same degree of consistency as the others, it does not have the same moderating effect on suicide.
[...]

But if religion preserves men from suicide simply because, and to the extent that, it constitutes a society, so too other societies probably have the same effect. Let us consider the family and political society from this perspective.

If one's attention is confined to absolute figures, then unmarried people seem to commit suicide less than the married. [...] Certainly, if one follows popular opinion and considers suicide to be an act of despair caused by the difficulties of existence, this opinion appears plausible. The unmarried person does in fact have an easier life than the married. Is it not true that marriage entails all sorts of burdens and responsibilities? In order to preserve the family in the present and for the future, does it not require more sacrifices and suffering than it takes to meet the needs of an unmarried person? However obvious this may seem, such *a priori* reasoning is completely false and only seems to be supported by the facts because they have been poorly analyzed [...] we must remember that a considerable number of the unmarried are less than 16 years old, while all the married are older. Up to the age of 16 the tendency towards suicide is very slight because of the age factor, without considering others. [...] The only way to avoid these difficulties is to calculate the rate of each group separately, at each age. With such procedures one might, for example, compare unmarried people aged from 25 to 30 years with married and widowed persons of the same age, and similarly for other periods; the effect of married status would thus be isolated from all the other factors and all its possible variations would be evident. [...]

Thus, when we say that the 'coefficient of preservation' of husbands aged 25 compared to unmarried men is 3, we mean that if the tendency to suicide of married persons of this age is represented by 1, that of unmarried people the same age must be represented by 3. Obviously, when the coefficient of preservation drops below unity, it really becomes a coefficient of aggravation.

The laws derived from these tables may be formulated thus:
(1) Too early marriages have an aggravating influence on suicide, especially for men. [...]
(2) From the age of 20 onwards married people of both sexes benefit from a coefficient of preservation in comparison with single people. [...]

(3) The coefficient of preservation of married people compared with single people varies according to sex. [. . .] We can say that the sex which is most favoured by marriage varies according to the society, and the extent of the difference between the rate of the two sexes itself varies depending on which sex is most favoured. [. . .]

(4) Widowhood reduces the coefficient of married people of both sexes, but usually it does not eliminate it completely. Widowed people kill themselves more often than married people, but in general less than single people.

The coefficient of preservation of widowed people, like that of married people, in comparison with unmarried people, varies with sex. [. . .] We can state in the same terms, therefore, that the more favoured sex in the state of widowhood varies according to the society, and the differences between the two sexes itself varies depending on which sex is most favoured.

Having established the facts, let us look for the explanations.

The immunity enjoyed by married people can only be attributed to one of the following two causes:

It may be due to the influence of the domestic environment. It would then be the influence of the family which would neutralize any suicidal tendency or would prevent it from being realized.

Or it may be due to what might be called matrimonial selection. Marriage in fact operates a sort of automatic selection in the population as a whole. Not everyone who wants to marry does so; there is little chance of creating a successful family if one does not possess certain qualities of health, fortune and morality. [. . .]

It is in the constitution of the family group, therefore, that we must discover the principal cause of the phenomonon we are studying.

But, however interesting this result may be, it requires further definition; for the family environment is made up of different elements. For both husband and wife the family includes: (1) the wife or husband; (2) the children. Is the beneficial effect of the family on the suicidal tendency due to the former or the latter? To put it another way, the family consists of two different forms of association: the conjugal group and the family group proper. These two social entities do not share the same origin or character, and as a result it is unlikely that they have the same effects. Whilst one derives from a contract and an elective affinity, the other springs from a natural phenomenon, consanguinity; the former unites two members of the same generation, the latter joins one generation to the next; the latter is as old as humanity, the former became organized at a relatively later date. [. . .]

One proof of the slight effect of marriage is the fact that the marriage rate has not changed very much since the first decades of the century, while suicide has tripled. [. . .]

But the slight effect of marriage is revealed particularly clearly in the case of women when it does not find its natural fulfilment in children. [. . .] In France, married but childless women commit suicide half again as often as unmarried women of the same age. We have already noted that generally the wife benefits less from family life than the husband. Now we can see the cause of this; taken by itself, conjugal life is harmful to the woman and aggravates her tendency to suicide.

If, nevertheless, most wives have appeared to enjoy a favourable coefficient of preservation, this is because childless households are the exception and consequently the presence of children remedies and reduces the bad effects of marriage in most cases. [. . .]

From [. . .] the preceding remarks it appears that marriage certainly has its own preservative effect against suicide. But it is very limited and of benefit to one sex only [. . .] (T)he fact remains that the family is the essential factor in the immunity of married people, that is, the family as the whole group of parents and children. Obviously, as husband and wife are members, they also share in producing this result, not as husband or wife, however, but as father or mother, as functionaries of the family association. If the disappearance of one increases the chances of the other committing suicide, it is not because the personal bonds that united them are broken, but because the family suffers a disaster, the shock of which is borne by the survivor. We shall reserve the special effect of marriage for a later study, but it can be said that domestic society, like religious society, acts as a powerful counter-agent against suicide.

This immunity even increases with the density of the family, that is with the increase in the number of its elements. [. . .] Our previous conclusion may thus be completed to read: just as the family is a strong safeguard against suicide, so the more strongly it is constituted the greater its protection.

If it had not been for the fact that statistics were so late in being developed, it would have been easy to show by the same method that this law applies to political societies. History teaches that suicide, which is generally rare in societies that are young in evolution and concentration, increases as societies disintegrate. [. . .] Major political upheavals are sometimes said to increase the number of suicides. But Morselli has proved conclusively that the facts contradict their view. All the revolutions which have occurred in France this century reduced the number of suicides at the time. [. . .] Great national wars have the same effect as political upheavals. [...]

These facts can be interpreted in only one way; namely, that major social upheavals and great popular wars rouse collective sentiments, stimulate a partisan spirit and patriotism, political and national faith, and by concentrating activity towards a single end, gives rise, temporarily at least, to a stronger integration of society. The beneficial influence that we have demonstrated is not due to the crisis but to the struggles it gives rise to. Because they force men to close ranks and confront the common danger, the individual thinks less of himself and more of the common cause. [...]

We have, therefore, successively established the following three propositions:

Suicide varies inversely with the degree of integration of religious society.

Suicide varies inversely with the degree of integration of domestic society.

Suicide varies inversely with the degree of integration of political society.

[...]

So we come to this general conclusion: suicide varies inversely with the degree of integration of the social groups to which the individual belongs.

But society cannot disintegrate unless the individual simultaneously detaches himself from social life, unless his own ends become more important than common ends, that is to say, unless his personality begins to predominate over the collective personality. The weaker the groups to which he belongs become, the less he depends on them, and consequently relies only on himself and recognizes no other rules of conduct than those based on private interests. So if we agree to call this state 'egoism', where the individual ego asserts itself to excess in the face of the social ego, and at its expense, we can call the particular type of suicide that results from excessive individualism 'egoistic'.

ALTRUISTIC SUICIDE

In the natural order, no good is without limits. A biological quality can fulfil the ends which it is required to serve only on condition that it does not exceed certain limits. The same is true for social phenomena. If, as we have just seen, excessive individualism leads to suicide, insufficient individualism produces the same effects. When man is detached from society, he can easily kill himself, and this is also the case when he is too strongly integrated in society.

It has sometimes been said that suicide was unknown in lower societies. Expressed in these terms, the assertion is incorrect. It is true that egoistic suicide, as we have just described it, does not appear to be very common there. But there is another type which is found there in an endemic state. [. . .]

Suicide is therefore very common among primitive peoples. But it displays special characteristics. All the facts just considered fall into one of the following three categories:

(1) Suicides of men approaching old age or stricken with illness.
(2) Suicides of women on the death of the husband.
(3) Suicides of followers or servants on the death of their leaders.

In all these cases where a person kills himself it is not because he takes upon himself the right to do so, but, on the contrary, because *it is his duty*. If he fails in this obligation, he is punished by being dishonoured and, most often, by religious sanctions. [. . .]

For society to oblige certain members to kill themselves, it must be the case that the individual personality counts for very little. Since, as soon as such a personality begins to be formed, the right to life is the first right to be accorded to it. It is suspended only in very exceptional circumstances, such as war. But this weak individuation can itself have only one cause. For the individual to occupy so small a place in collective life he must be almost totally absorbed into the group and, consequently, be very strongly integrated. For the parts to have so little life of their own, the whole must form a compact and continuous mass. In fact we have shown elsewhere that this massive cohesion is characteristic of societies where the preceding practices are observed. [. . .]

We are therefore confronted with a type of suicide that differs from the preceding one by virtue of certain specific qualities. Whilst the latter is caused by excessive individuation, for the former it is insufficient individuation. [. . .] Having designated as 'egoism' the condition in which the ego pursues its own life and is obedient only to itself, the designation 'altruism' adequately expresses the opposite condition, where the ego is not its own property. It is blended with something other than itself, and the goal of conduct is external to itself, that is, in one of the groups in which it participates. Thus we call the suicide caused by intense altruism 'altruistic suicide'. But as it is also characteristically carried out as a duty, the designation should express this fact. So we will designate such a type 'obligatory altruistic suicide'.

It needs to be defined by the combination of these two adjectives, because not every altruistic suicide is necessarily obligatory. Some are not imposed by society so directly, having a more optional character. [. . .] The willingness of the Japanese to disembowel themselves for the slightest reason is well known. [. . .] A social prestige thus attaches to suicide, which is encouraged by this fact, and to decline this reward has effects similar to punishment. [. . .] But it even happens that the individual kills himself purely for the joy of sacrifice, despite the absence of a specific reason, because renunciation is itself considered praiseworthy. India provides the classic ground for this sort of suicide. The Hindu was predisposed to self-destruction under Brahminic influence. [. . .]

Thus we have constructed a second type of suicide, which itself consists of three forms: obligatory altruistic suicide, optional altruistic suicide, and acute altruistic suicide, the pure form of which is mystical suicide. [. . .]

Such suicides are unlikely to occur very widely in our own contemporary societies, where individual personality is increasingly freed from the collective personality. It cannot be denied that some people may have yielded to altruistic motives, such as soldiers who have preferred death to the humiliation of defeat [. . .] or those sad people who kill themselves to avoid disgracing their family. When such people renounce life it is on account of something they love better than themselves. But these are isolated and exceptional cases, although there still exists a contemporary setting where altruistic suicide is chronic: specifically, the army.

In all European societies it is in fact generally the case that the suicidal propensity of soldiers is far higher than that of civilians of the same age. [. . .] Among all the components of modern society, it is the army that most resembles the structure of lower societies. It, too, constitutes a massive, compact group, which provides a rigid setting for the individual, and prevents any independent movement.

ANOMIC SUICIDE

But society is not simply something that attracts the sentiments and activities of individuals with unequalled force. It is also a power that controls them. There is a relationship between the way in which this regulating action is performed and the social suicide-rate.

The fact that economic crises have an aggravating effect on the suicide tendency is well-known. [. . .] But to what do these crises owe their influence? Is life more readily renounced as it becomes more difficult? This explanation is attractively simple; and it fits in with the popular idea of suicide. But it is contradicted by the facts. [. . .]

Rather than an increase in poverty causing an increase in suicide, it is more the case that even fortunate crises, which have the effect of abruptly raising a country's prosperity, have an effect on suicide like economic disasters. [. . .] What proves even more conclusively that economic distress does not have the aggravating effect often attributed to it, is that it tends to give rise to exactly the opposite effect. [. . .] Poverty may even be considered a protection. In various French regions, those which have more people with independent means have higher numbers of suicides.

Thus, if industrial or financial crises increase suicides, it is not because they cause poverty, since crises of prosperity have the same result; rather, it is because they are crises, in other words, disturbances of the collective order. Every disturbance of equilibrium, even though it may involve greater comfort and a raising of the general pace of life, provides an impulse to voluntary death. [. . .]

No living person can be happy or even continue to exist if his needs are not sufficiently in proportion to his means. Otherwise, whether they require more than can be granted, or simply something different, those needs will be in constant conflict and bring only pain. Any action that cannot take place without pain tends not to be reproduced. Tendencies which are not satisfied atrophy, and since the tendency to live is simply the result of all the others, it cannot but weaken if other tendencies diminish. [. . .]

Human nature in itself cannot set variable limits to our needs. Consequently, in so far as it is left to the individual alone, these needs are unlimited. Without reference to any external regulating influence, our capacity for sensation is a bottomless abyss that nothing can satisfy.

But, then, if nothing external manages to restrict this capacity, it can only be a source of torment to itself. Unlimited desires are insatiable by definition, and insatiability is rightly considered a pathological symptom. [. . .]

Society alone can perform this moderating role, either directly and as a whole, or through the agency of one of its organs; for it is the only moral power superior to the individual, whose authority he accepts. [. . .] When society is disturbed, either by a painful crisis or by favourable, but abrupt, changes, it is temporarily incapable of exercising this action; and it is then that we get those sudden rises in the curve of suicides that were noted earlier.

In fact, in the case of economic disasters, a sort of declassification occurs whereby certain individuals are suddenly thrust into a lower position than they formerly occupied. They must then reduce their requirements, restrain their needs and learn to control themselves more. All the benefits of social influence are lost as far as they are concerned; their moral education has to begin again. Society cannot immediately adapt them to this new existence or teach them to exercise the additional restraint to which they are not accustomed. [. . .]

But the same applies if the crisis originates in a sudden increase in power and fortune. In this case, as the conditions of life are changed, the scale which regulated needs can no longer remain the same; for it varies according to social resources, since it largely determines the share of each class of producers. The scale is upset, but on the other hand, a new scale cannot be quickly improvised. It takes time for men and things to be reclassified by the public consciousness. As long as these liberated social forces have not regained their equilibrium, their respective values remain undetermined and therefore regulation is lacking for a while. One no longer knows what is fair, what are legitimate claims and hopes, and which are excessive. As a result, there is nothing to which one does not aspire. If this is a deep disturbance, it affects even the principles that regulate the distribution of different jobs between people. Since the relations between the various parts of society are necessarily changed, the ideas that express these relations must change. Any class that the crisis has particularly favoured is no longer resigned to its lot and, on the other hand, its good fortune awakens all sorts of jealousies above and below it. Appetites no longer accept limits on behaviour, since public opinion cannot restrain them. At the same time they are in a state of abnormal excitement simply because of the greater intensity of life in general. [. . .] This state of deregulation or 'anomie' is therefore further heightened by the fact that passions are less disciplined at the very moment when they need stronger discipline. [. . .]

If anomie never occurred except in intermittent spurts, as in the earlier cases, and in acute crises, it might well cause the social suicide-rate to vary from time to time; but it would not be a regular constant factor. There is a sphere of life, however, where it is at present in a chronic state: the world of trade and industry.

For a century economic progress has mainly consisted of freeing industrial relations from regulations. Until recent times, it was the function of a whole system of moral forces to discipline them. First, there was religion, the influence of which was felt equally by workers and employers, poor and rich. It consoled the former and taught them to be content with their lot, stating that the social order was providential, that each class's share was fixed by God Himself, and by making them hope for compensation for present inequalities in a world to come. It restrained the latter by reminding them that earthly interests are not everything for man, that they must be subordinate to other, higher interests, and that in conesquence they should not be pursued without regulation or to excess. Temporal power, for its part, moderated the scope of economic functions by its supremacy over them and the relatively subordinate position it gave them. At the heart of the business world itself, the occupational groups, by regulating salaries, prices and production, indirectly fixed the average level of income on which needs are partly based by the very force of circumstances. In describing this organization, we do not mean to propose it as a model. It is clear that, without profound changes, it would be inappropriate for present-day societies. All we are saying is that it existed, that it had useful effects, and that nothing has yet taken its place.

The reality is that religion has lost most of its power. And governmental power, rather than regulating economic life, has become its instrument and servant. Opposing schools of thought, such as orthodox economists and extreme socialists are in agreement about reducing it to a more or less passive role as intermediary between various social functions. The former want to make it simply the guardian of individual contracts; the latter expect it to attend to collective accounting, that is, to record consumer demands and transmit them to producers, to make an inventory of total income and redistribute it according to an established formula. But both refuse it power to subordinate other social organs to itself and to make them converge towards a single dominant aim. For both sides, nations are supposed to have as their only or principal objective the achievement of industrial prosperity; this is the implication of the dogma of economic materialism basic to both systems of thought, which are opposite only in appearance. As these theories merely express existing opinion, industry, instead of continuing to be regarded as a means to an end which transcends it, has become the supreme end for individuals and society. But then appetites thus awakened are freed from any limiting authority. By sanctifying these appetites, so to sepak, this deification of material well-being has placed them above all human law. Restraining them seems like a kind of sacrilege. [. . .]

This is the reason for the excitement which predominates in this part of society, but which has spread to all the rest. A constant state of crisis and anomie exists there. From the top to the bottom of the scale, covetous desires are aroused without it being known where they might level out. [. . .]

Industrial and commercial functions are amongst the occupations which furnish the greatest number of suicides. They almost reach the level of the liberal professions, indeed they sometimes exceed it; they are certainly more affected than agriculture. The case of agriculture provides the best reminder of the constitution of the economic order as it used to be. The difference would be even more marked if, among industrial suicides, we distinguished beween employers and workers, for it is probably the former who are most affected by the condition to anomie. The high rate for those with independent means (720 per million) shows clearly that it is the better off who suffer most. This is because everything that enforces subordination reduces the effects of this condition. The lower classes have their horizon limited by those above them, and because of that their desires are more restrained. But those who have only empty space above them are almost inevitably lost in it, unless there is some force to hold them back.

Anomie, therefore, is a regular and specific factor in causing suicide in our modern societies. it is one of the sources feeding the annual totals. This is a new type that must be distinguished from the others. It differs from them in that it does not depend on the way in which individuals are attached to society, but on the way in which they are regulated by society. Egoistic suicide stems from the fact that men no longer see a reason for living; altruisitic suicide comes from the fact that this reason appears to them to lie outside life itself; the third kind of suicide, whose existence we have just established, comes from the fact that their activity is unregulated and they suffer as a consequence. Because of its origin, we shall call this last type 'anomic suicide'.

Certainly this type and egoistic suicide have ties of kinship. Both come from society's insufficient presence in individuals. But the sphere of its absence is not the same in both cases. In egoistic suicide society is deficient in truly collective activity, thus leaving it deprived of objects and meaning. In anomic suicide society has a weak presence in the really individual passions, leaving them without a restraining influence. The result is that, despite their ties, these two types remain independent of each other. We can offer to society everything social in us, but still be unable to limit our desires; without being an egoist one can live in a state of anomie, and vice versa. These two types of suicide do not draw their recruits from the same social environments; one has its main location in the intellectual occupations, the world of thought, the other is in the industrial or commercial world.

But economic anomie is not the only anomie that can lead to suicide.

[. . .] (T)hroughout Europe the number of suicides varies with that of divorces and separations. [. . .] One must seek the cause of this remarkable relationship, not in the predispositions of people's mental character, but in the intrinsic nature of divorce. At this point we may state as our first proposition: in all countries for which we have the necessary data, suicides of divorced people are extremely more numerous than those of other sections of the population. [. . .] What is the explanation? [. . .]

With regard to suicide, the more widely practised divorce is, the more marriage favours the wife and vice versa. [. . .]

Two consequences follow from this proposition.

The first is that only husbands contribute to the rise in the suicide rate in societies where divorce is frequent; by contrast, wives commit suicide less in those circumstances than elsewhere. If, therefore, divorce only develops in association with an improvement in women's moral situation, it cannot be accepted that divorce is linked to domestic society being in such a bad condition that it increases the tendency to suicide, for this increase would then occur for both husbands and wives. A weakening of the family spirit cannot have such opposite effects on the two sexes, on the one hand proving favourable to the mother but on the other hand having a serious effect on the father. Consequently, it is within the state of marriage and not of the family that the cause is to be found of the phenomenon we are studying. In fact, it is very likely that marriage acts in opposite ways on husband and wife. As parents they have the same objective, but as partners their interests are different and often opposed. It may well be the case that, in certain societies, particular aspects of the institution of marriage may benefit one and harm the other. Everything we have seen tends to prove that this is precisely the case with divorce.

Secondly, the same reason leads us to reject the hypothesis that this unfortunate state of marriage, to which divorce and suicide are closely related, derives from a greater frequency of matrimonial disputes; for such a cause should not result in increasing the wife's immunity any more than the weakening of family ties. If, where divorce is common, the suicide figures were really related to the number of conjugal quarrels, the wife should suffer as much as the husband. There is nothing in this situation which could give her special protection. Such a hypothesis is that much less tenable because divorce is more often asked for by the wife than by the husband (in 60% of French divorces and 83% of separations). So domestic disturbances are attributable to the man in the majority of cases. Hence, it would not be clear why, in countries where divorce is common, it is the man who commits suicide more frequently when it is he who causes more suffering to the wife, whilst the wife is less likely to commit suicide when her husband causes her to suffer more. Moreover, it has not been proved that the number of marriage quarrels increases in proportion to the number of divorces.

If we do not accept this hypothesis, there is only one other that is possible. The very institution of divorce, though its effect on marriage, must be the determining factor in suicide.

And what, in fact, is marriage? A regulation of relationships between the sexes, which extends not only to physical instincts that are active, but also to all kinds of feelings that civilization has gradually grafted on to the foundation of physical appetites. [. . .] By fixing the conjugal state for ever, it allows no way out and forbids all hopes, even legitimate ones. Even the man suffers from this immutability; but the disadvantages for him are largely compensated for by the advantages which he gains in other respects. Moreover, custom grants the man certain privileges which allow him to alleviate the rigour of the regime to some extent. On the other hand, for the woman there is neither compensation nor alleviation. For her, monogamy is a strict obligation. [. . .]

We thus come to the conclusion that is rather far removed from current ideas about marriage and its role. It is supposed to have been instituted for the benefit of the wife to protect her weakness against male capriciousness. Monogamy, particularly, is often presented as a sacrifice of man's polygamous instincts that he makes in order to raise and improve women's condition in marriage. In reality, whatever might have been the historical causes which made him impose this restriction, it is the man who benefits from it. The freedom that he has given up can thus only be a source of torment for him. The woman does not have the same reasons to give it up and, in this respect, one might say that, by submitting to the same rules, it is she who has made the sacrifice.[1]

---

[1] From these considerations we can see that there is a type of suicide that is the opposite of anomic suicide, just as egoistic and altruistic suicide are opposites. This one results from excessive regulation; the type committed by people whose future is mercilessly blocked, whose passions are violently suppressed by an oppressive discipline. It is the suicide of very young husbands, of the childless married woman. To complete the picture, we must therefore establish a fourth type of suicide. But it is so unimportant today, and it is so very difficult to find examples other than the ones quoted, that it seems pointless to dwell on it. Yet it could be of historical interest. Are not slave suicides, which are thought to be common in certain circumstances (V. Corre, *Le Crime en pays créoles,* p. 48) and, in fact, all those suicides attributable to excesses of physical or moral despotism, examples of this type? To bring out the ineluctable, inflexible character of the rule which cannot be changed, and in contrast to the expression 'anomie' that we have been using, we might call this 'fatalistic suicide'.

THE SOCIAL ELEMENT OF SUICIDE

As a consequence of seeking the causes of the suicide tendency of each society in the nature of the societies themselves, and by leaving aside the individual, we have obtained completely different results. Whereas the relationships between suicide and biological or physical factors were uncertain and ambiguous, those between suicide and certain sorts of social environment were direct and constant. It is here that we finally encountered real laws, allowing us to attempt a methodical classification of types of suicide. [. . .]

From all these facts we can conclude that the social suicide rate can only be explained sociologically. It is the moral constitution of the society which always determines the quota of voluntary deaths. For each population there is a collective force with a particular strength which impels men to kill themselves.

Part Five

Religion and Knowledge

THE ELEMENTARY FORMS
OF THE RELIGIOUS LIFE

[. . .]

The study which we are undertaking is therefore a way of taking up again, *but under new conditions,* the old problem of the origin of religion. To be sure, if by origin we are to understand the very first beginning, the question has nothing scientific about it, and should be resolutely discarded. [. . .]

What we want to do is to find a means of discerning the ever-present causes upon which the most essential forms of religious thought and practice depend. [. . .]

For a long time it has been known that the first systems of representations with which men have pictured to themselves the world and themselves were of religious origin. There is no religion that is not a cosmology at the same time that it is a speculation upon divine things. If philosophy and the sciences were born of religion, it is because religion began by taking the place of the sciences and philosophy. But it has been less frequently noticed that religion has not confined itself

Edited and reprinted with permission from: *The Elementary Forms of the Religious Life,* 1915. Translated by J. W. Swain. London, Allen & Unwin, pp.8–11, 37–44, 47, 205–207, 209–215, 228–229, 231–232, 417–424, 427–431. Reproduced by permission of the publishers, London, Allen & Unwin, and New York, The Free Press.

to enriching the human intellect, formed beforehand, with a certain number of ideas; it has contributed to forming the intellect itself. Men owe to it not only a good part of the substance of their knowledge, but also the form in which this knowledge has been elaborated.

At the roots of all our judgments there are a certain number of essential ideas which dominate all our intellectual life; they are what philosophers since Aristotle have called the categories of the understanding: ideas of time, space, class, number, cause, substance, personality, etc. They correspond to the most universal properties of things. They are like the solid frame which encloses all thought; this does not seem to be able to liberate itself from them without destroying itself, for it seems that we cannot think of objects that are not in time and space, which have no number, etc. Other ideas are contingent and unsteady; we can conceive of their being unknown to a man, a society or an epoch; but these others appear to be nearly inseparable from the normal working of the intellect. They are like the framework of the intelligence. Now when primitive religious beliefs are systematically analysed, the principal categories are naturally found. They are born in religion and of religion; they are a product of religious thought. This is a statement that we are going to have occasion to make many times in the course of this work.

This remark has some interest of itself already; but here is what gives it its real importance.

The general conclusion of the book which the reader has before him is that religion is something eminently social. Religious representations are collective representations which express collective realities; the rites are a manner of acting which take rise in the midst of the assembled groups and which are destined to excite, maintain or recreate certain mental states in these groups. So if the categories are of religious origin, they ought to participate in this nature common to all religious facts; they too should be social affairs and the product of collective thought. At least — for in the actual condition of our knowledge of these matters, one should be careful to avoid all radical and exclusive statements — it is allowable to suppose that they are rich in social elements.

Even at present, these can be imperfectly seen in some of them. For example, try to represent what the notion of time would be without the processes by which we divide it, measure it or express it with objective signs, a time which is not a succession of years, weeks, days and hours! This is something nearly unthinkable. We cannot conceive of time, except on condition of distinguishing its different moments. Now what is the origin of this differentiation? Undoubtedly, the states of consciousness which we have already experienced can be reproduced in us in the same order in which they passed in the first place; thus portions of our past become present again, though being clearly distinguished from the present. But howsoever important this distinction may be for our private experience, it is far from being enough to constitute the notion or category of time. This does not consist merely in a commemoration, either partial or integral, of our past life. It is an abstract and impersonal frame which surrounds, not only our individual existence, but that of all humanity. It is like an endless chart, where all duration is spread out before the mind, and upon which all possible events can be located in relation to fixed and determined guide lines. It is not *my time* that is thus arranged; it is time in general, such as it is objectively thought of by everybody in a single civilization. That alone is enough to give us a hint that such an arrangement ought to be collective. And in reality, observation proves that these indispensable guide lines, in relation to which all things are temporily located, are taken from social life. The divisions into days, weeks, months, years, etc., correspond to the periodical recurrence of rites, feasts, and public ceremonies. A calendar expresses the rhythm of the collective activities, while at the same time its function is to assure their regularity.

It is the same thing with space. [. . .]

All known religious beliefs, whether simple or complex, present one common characteristic: they presuppose a classification of all the things, real and ideal, of which men think, into two classes or opposed groups, generally designated by two distinct terms which are translated well enough by the words *profane* and *sacred (profane, sacré)*. This division of the world into two domains, the one containing all that is sacred, the other all that is profane, is the distinctive trait of religious thought; the beliefs, myths, dogmas and legends are either representations or systems of representations which express the nature of sacred things, the virtues and powers which are attributed to them, or their relations with each other and with profane things. [. . .]

But if a purely hierarchic distinction is a criterium [sic] at once too general and too imprecise, there is nothing left with which to characterize the sacred in its relation to the profane except their heterogeneity. However, this heterogeneity is sufficient to characterize this classification of things and to distinguish it from all others, because it is very particular: *it is absolute*. In all the history of human thought there exists no other example of two categories of things so profoundly differentiated or so radically opposed to one another. The traditional opposition of good and bad is nothing beside this; for the good and the bad are only two opposed species of the same class, namely morals, just as sickness and health are two different aspects of the same order of facts, life, while the sacred and the profane have always and everywhere been conceived by the human mind as two distinct classes, as two worlds between which there is nothing in common. The foces which play in one are not simply those which are met with in the other, but a little stronger; they are of a different sort. [. . .]

Thus we arrive at the first criterium [sic] of religious beliefs. Undoubtedly there are secondary species within these two fundamental classes which, in their turn, are more or less incompatible with each other, But the real characteristic of religious phenomena is that they always suppose a bipartite division of the whole universe, known and knowable, into two classes which embrace all that exists, but which radically exclude each other. Sacred things are those which the interdictions protect and isolate; profane things, those to which these interdictions are applied and which must remain at a distance from the first. Religious beliefs are the representations which express the nature of sacred things and the relations which they sustain, either with each other or with profane things. Finally, rites are the rules of conduct which prescribe how a man should comport himself in the presence of these sacred objects. [. . .]

However, this definition is not yet complete, for it is equally applicable to two sorts of facts which, while being related to each other, must be distinguished nevertheless: these are magic and religion.

Magic, too, is made up of beliefs and rites. Like religion, it has its myths and its dogmas; only they are more elementary, undoubtedly because, seeking technical and utilitarian ends, it does not waste its time in pure speculation. [. . .]

Here is how a line of demarcation can be traced between these two domains.

The really religious beliefs are always common to a determined group, which makes profession of adhering to them and of practising the rites connected with them. They are not merely received individually by all the members of this group; they are something belonging to the group, and they make its unity. The individuals which compose it feel themselves united to each other by the simple fact that they have a common faith. A society whose members are united by the fact that they think in the same way in regard to the sacred world and its relations with the profane world, and by the fact that they translate these common ideas into common practices, is what is called a Church.

[. . .]

It is quite another matter with magic. To be sure, the belief in magic is always more or less general; it is very frequently diffused in large masses of the population, and there are even peoples where it has as many adherents as the real religion. But it does not result in binding together those who adhere to it, nor in uniting them into a group leading a common life. *There is no Church of magic.* Between the magician and the individuals who consult him, as between these individuals themselves, there are no lasting bonds which make them members of the same moral community, comparable to that formed by the believers in the same god or the observers of the same cult. The magician has a clientele and not a Church, and it is very possible that his clients have no other relations between each other, or even do not know each other; even the relations which they have with him are generally accidental and transient; they are just like those of a sick man with his physician. [. . .]

Thus we arrive at the following definition: *A religion is a unified system of beliefs and practices relative to sacred things, that is to say, things set apart and forbidden — beliefs and practices which unite into one single moral community called a Church, all those who adhere to them.* The second element which thus finds a place in our definition is no less essential than the first; for by showing that the idea of religion is inseparable from that of the Church, it makes it clear that religion should be an eminently collective thing.

ORIGIN OF THE IDEA OF THE TOTEMIC PRINCIPLE OR MANA

The proposition established in the preceding chapter determines the terms in which the problem of the origins of totemism should be posed. Since totemism is everywhere dominated by the idea of quasi-divine principle, immanent in certain categories of men and things and thought of under the form of an animal or vegetable, the explanation of this religion is essentially the explanation of this belief; to arrive at this, we must seek to learn how men who have been led to construct this idea and out of what materials they have constructed it.

It is obviously not out of the sensations which the things serving as totems are able to arouse in the mind; we have shown that these things are frequently insignificant. [. . .]

Thus the totem is before all a symbol, a material expression of something else. But of what?

From the analysis to which we have been giving our attention, it is evident that it expresses and symbolizes two different sorts of things. In the first place, it is the outward and visible form of what we have called the totemic principle or god. But it is also the symbol of the determined society called the clan. It is its flag; it is the sign by which each clan distinguishes itself from the others, the visible mark of its personality, a mark borne by everything which is a part of the clan under any title whatsoever, men, beasts or things. So if it is at once the symbol of the god and of the society, is that not because the god and the society are only one? How could the emblem of the group have been able to become the figure of this quasi-divinity, if the group and the divinity were two distinct realities? The god of the clan, the totemic principle, can therefore be nothing else than the clan itself, personified and represented to the imagination under the visible form of the animal or vegetable which serves as totem.

But how has this apotheosis been possible, and how did it happen to take place in this fashion?

In a general way, it is unquestionable that a society has all that is necessary to arouse the sensation of the divine in minds, merely by the power that it has over them; for to its members it is what a god is to his worshippers. In fact, a god is, first of all, a being whom men think of as superior to themselves, and upon whom they feel that they depend. Whether it be a conscious personality, such as Zeus or Jahveh, or merely abstract forces such as those in play in totemism, the worshipper, in the one case as in the other, believes himself held to certain manners of acting which are imposed upon him by the nature of the sacred principle with which he feels that he is in communion. Now society also gives us the sensation of a perpetual dependence. Since it has a nature which is peculiar to itself and different from our individual nature, it pursues ends which are likewise special to it; but, as it cannot attain them except through out intermediacy, it imperiously demands our aid. It requires that, forgetful of our own interest, we make ourselves its servitors, and it submits us to every sort of inconvenience, privation and sacrifice, without which social life would be impossible. It is because of this that at every instant we are obliged to submit ourselves to rules of conduct and of thought which we have neither made nor desired, and which are sometimes even contrary to our most fundamental inclination and instincts.

Even if society were unable to obtain these concessions and sacrifices from us except by a material constraint, it might awaken in us only the idea of a physical force to which we must give way of necessity, instead of that of a moral power such as religions adore. But as a matter of fact, the empire which it holds over consciences is due much less to the physical supremacy of which it has the privilege than to the moral authority with which it is invested. If we yield to its orders, it is not merely because it is strong enough to triumph over our resistance;

it is primarily because it is the object of a venerable respect.

We say that an object, whether individual or collective, inspires respect when the representation expressing it in the mind is gifted with such a force that it automatically causes or inhibits actions, *without regard for any consideration relative to their useful or injurious effects*. When we obey somebody because of the moral authority which we recognize in him, we follow out his opinions, not because they seem wise, but because a certain sort of physical energy is immanent in the idea that we form of this person, which conquers our will and inclines it in the indicated direction. Respect is the emotion which we experience when we feel this interior and wholly spiritual pressure operating upon us. [. . .]

Since it is in spiritual ways that social pressure exercises itself, it could not fail to give men the idea that outside themselves there exist one or several powers, both moral and, at the same time, efficacious, upon which they depend. They must think of these powers, at least in part, as outside themselves, for these address them in a tone of command and sometimes even order them to do violence to their most natural inclinations. It is undoubtedly true that if they were able to see that these influences which they feel emanate from society, then the mythological system of interpretations would never be born. But social action follows ways that are too circuitous and obscure, and employs psychical mechanisms that are too complex to allow the ordinary observer to see when it comes. As long as scientific analysis does not come to teach it to them, men know well that they are acted upon, but they do no know by whom. So they must invent by themselves the idea of these powers with which they feel themselves in connection, and from that, we are able to catch a glimpse of the way by which they were led to represent them under forms that are really foreign to their nature and to transfigure them by thought.

But a god is not merely an authority upon whom we depend; it is a force upon which our strength relies. The man who has obeyed his god and who for this reason, believes the god is with him, approaches the world with confidence and with the feeling of an increased energy. Likewise, social action does not confine itself to demanding sacrifices, privations and efforts from us. For the collective force is not entirely outside of us; it does not act upon us wholly from without; but rather, since society cannot exist except in and through individual consciousness, this force must also penetrate us and organize itself within us; it thus becomes an integral part of our being and by that very fact this is elevated and magnified.

There are occasions when this strengthening and vivifying action of society is especially apparent. In the midst of an assembly animated by a common passion, we become susceptible of acts and sentiments of which we are incapable when reduced to our own forces; and when the assembly is dissolved and when, finding ourselves alone again, we fall back to our ordinary level, we are then able to measure the height to which we have been raised above ourselves. History abounds in examples of this sort. [. . .]

Besides these passing and intermittent states, there are other more durable ones, where this strengthening influence of society makes itself felt with greater consequences and frequently even with greater brilliancy. There are periods in history when, under the influence of some great collective shock, social interactions have become much more frequent and active. Men look for each other and assemble together more than ever. That general effervescence results which is characteristic of revolutionary or creative epochs. [. . .]

Also, in the present day just as much as in the past, we see society constantly creating sacred things out of ordinary ones. If it happens to fall in love with a man and if it thinks it has found in him the principal aspirations that move it, as well as the means of satisfying them, this man will be raised above the others and, as it were, deified. Opinion will invest him with a majesty exactly analogous to that protecting the gods. This is what has happened to so many sovereigns in whom their age had faith: if they were not made gods, they were at least regarded as direct representatives of the deity. And the fact that it is society alone which is the author of these varieties of apotheosis, is evident since it frequently chances to consecrate men thus who have no right to it from their own merit. The simple deference inspired by men invested with high social functions is not different in nature from religious respect. It is expressed by the same movements: a man keeps at a distance from a high personage; he approaches him only with precautions; in conversing with him, he uses other gestures and language than those used with ordinary mortals. The sentiment felt on these occasions is so closely related to the religious sentiment that many peoples have confounded the two.

In addition to men, society also consecrates things, especially ideas. If a belief is unanimously shared by a people, then, for the reason which we pointed out above, it is forbidden to touch it, that is to say, to deny it or to contest it. Now the prohibition of criticism is an interdiction like the others and proves the presence of something sacred. Even to-day, howsoever great may be the liberty which we accord to others, a man who should totally deny progress or ridicule the human ideal to which modern societies are attached, would produce the effect of a sacrilege. There is at least one principle which those the most devoted to the free examination of everything tend to place above discussion and to regard as untouchable, that is to say, as sacred: this is the very principle of free examination.

All these facts allow us to catch glimpses of how the clan was able to awaken within its members the idea that outside of them there exist forces which dominate them and at the same time sustain them, that is to say in fine, religious forces: it is because there is no society with which the primitive is more directly and closely connected. The bonds uniting him to the tribe are much more lax and more feebly felt. Although this is not at all strange or foreign to him, it is with the people of his own clan that he has the greater number of things in common; it is the action of this group that he feels the most directly; so it is this also which, in preference to all others, should express itself in religious symbols.

The life of the Australian societies passes alternately through two distinct phases. Sometimes the population is broken up into little groups who wander about independently of one another, in their various occupations; each family lives by itself, hunting and fishing, and in a word, trying to procure its indispensable food by all the means in its power. Sometimes, on the contrary, the population concentrates and gathers at determined points for a length of time varying from several days to several months. This concentration takes place when a clan or a part of the tribe is summoned to the gathering, and on this occasion they celebrate a religious ceremony, or else hold what is called a corrobbori in the usual ethnological language.

These two phases are contrasted with each other in the sharpest way. In the first, economic activity is the preponderating one, and it is generally of a very mediocre intensity. Gathering the grains or herbs that are necessary for food, or hunting and fishing are not occupations to awaken very lively passions. The dispersed condition in which the society finds itself results in making its life uniform, languishing and dull. But when a corrobbori takes place, everything changes. Since the emotional and passional faculties of the primitive are only imperfectly placed under the control of his reason and will, he easily loses control of himself. Any event of some importance puts him quite outside himself. [. . .]

We are now able to understand how the totemic principle, and in general, every religious force, comes to be outside of the object in which it resides. It is because the idea of it is in no way made up of the impressions directly produced by this thing upon our senses or minds. Religious force is only the sentiment inspired by the group in its members, but projected outside of the consciousnesses that experience them, and objectified. To be objectified, they are fixed upon some object which thus becomes sacred; but any object might fulfil this function. In principle, there are none whose nature predestines them to it to the exclusion of all others; but also there are none that are necessarily impossible. Everything depends upon the circumstances which lead the sentiment creating religious ideas to establish itself here or there, upon this point or upon that one. Therefore, the sacred character assumed by an object is not implied in the intrinsic properties of this latter: *it is added to them.* The world of religious things is not one particular aspect of empirical nature; *it is superimposed upon it.* [...]

Thus social life, in all its aspects and in every period of its history, is made possible only by a vast symbolism. The material emblems and figurative representations with which we are more especially concerned in our present study, are one form of this; but there are many others. Collective sentiments can just as well become incarnate in persons or formulae: some formulae are flags, while there are persons, either real or mythical, who are symbols. [...]

Our entire study rests upon this postulate that the unanimous sentiment of the believers of all times cannot be purely illusory. Together with a recent apologist of the faith we admit that these religious beliefs rest upon a specific experience whose demonstrative value is, in one sense, not one bit inferior to that of scientific experiments, though different from them. We, too, think that 'a tree is known by its fruits,' and that fertility is the best proof of what the roots are worth. But from the fact that a 'religious experience,' if we choose to call it this, does exist and that it has a certain foundation – and, by the way, is there any experience which has none? – it does not follow that the reality which is its foundation conforms objectively to the idea which believers have of it. The very fact that the fashion in which it has been conceived has varied infinitely in different times is enough to prove that none of these conceptions express it adequately. If a scientist states it as an axiom that the sensations of heat and light which we feel correspond to some objective cause, he does not conclude that this is what it appears to the senses to be. Likewise, even if the impressions which the faithful feel are not imaginary, still they are in no way privileged institutions; there is no reason for believing that they inform us better upon the nature of their object than do ordinary sensations upon the nature of bodies and their properties. In order to discover what this object consists of, we must submit them to an examination and elaboration analogous to that which has substituted for the sensuous idea of the world another which is scientific and conceptual.

This is precisely what we have tried to do, and we have seen that this reality, which mythologies have represented under so many different forms, but which is the universal and eternal objective cause of these sensations *sui generis* out of which religious experience is made, is society. We have shown what moral forces it develops and how it awakens this sentiment of a refuge, of a shield and of a guardian support which attaches the believer to his cult. It is that which raises him outside himself; it is even that which made him. For that which makes a man is the totality of the intellectual property which constitutes civilization, and civilization is the work of society. This is explained [by] the preponderating rôle of the cult in all religions, whichever they may be. This is because society cannot make its influence felt unless it is in action, and it is not in action unless the individuals who compose it are assembled together and act in common. It is by common action that it takes consciousness of itself and realizes its position; it is before all else an active co-operation. The collective ideas and sentiments are even possible only owing to these exterior movements which symbolize them, as we have established. Then it is action which dominates the religious life, because of the mere fact that it is society which is its source.

In addition to all the reasons which have been given to justify this conception, a final one may be added here, which is the result of our whole work. As we have progressed, we have established the fact that the fundamental categories of thought, and consequently of science, are of religious origin. We have seen that the same is true for magic and consequently for the different processes which have issued from it. On the other hand, it has long been known that up until a relatively advanced moment of evolution, moral and legal rules have been indistinguishable from ritual prescriptions. In summing up, then, it may be said that nearly all the great social institutions have been born in religion. Now in order that these principal aspects of the collective life may have commenced by being only varied aspects of the religious life, it is obviously necessary that the religious life be the eminent form and, as it were, the concentrated expression of the whole collective life. If religion has given birth to all that is essential in society, it is because the idea of society is the soul of religion. [. . .]

But, it is said, what society is it that has thus made the basis of religion? Is it the real society, such as it is and acts before our very eyes, with the legal and moral organization which it has laboriously fashioned during the course of history? This is full of defects and imperfections. In it, evil goes beside the good, injustice often reigns supreme, and the truth is often obscured by error. How could anything so crudely organized inspire the sentiments of love, the ardent enthusiasm and the spirit of abnegation which all religions claim of their followers? These perfect beings which are gods could not have taken their traits from so mediocre, and sometimes even so base a reality.

But, on the other hand, does someone think of a perfect society, where justice and truth would be sovereign, and from which evil in all its forms would be banished for ever? No one would deny that this is in close relations with the religious sentiment; for, they would say, it is towards the realization of this that all religions strive. But that society is not an empirical fact, definite and observable; it is a fancy, a dream with which men have lightened their sufferings, but in which they have never really lived. It is merely an idea which comes to express our more or less obscure aspirations towards the good, the beautiful and the ideal. Now these aspirations have their roots in us; they come from the very depths of our being; then there is nothing outside of us which can account for them. Moreover, they are already religious in themselves; thus it would seem that the ideal society presupposes religion, far from being able to explain it.

But, in the first place, things are arbitrarily simplified when religion is seen only on its idealistic side: in its way, it is realistic. There is no physical or moral ugliness, there are no vices or evils which do not have a special divinity. There are gods of theft and trickery, of lust and war, of sickness and of death. Christianity itself, howsoever high the idea which it has made of the divinity may be, has been obliged to give the spirit of evil a place in its mythology. Satan is an essential piece of the Christian system; even if he is an impure being, he is not a profane one. The anti-god is a god, inferior and subordinated, it is true, but nevertheless endowed with extended powers; he is even the object of rites, at least of negative ones. Thus religion, far from ignoring the real society and making abstraction of it, is in its image; it reflects all its aspects, even the most vulgar and the most repulsive. All is to be found there, and if in the majority of cases we see the good victorious over evil, life over death, the powers of light over powers of darkness, it is because reality is not otherwise. If the relation between these two contrary forces were reversed, life would be impossible; but, as a matter of fact, it maintains itself and even tends to develop.

But if, in the midst of these mythologies and theologies we see reality clearly appearing, it is none the less true that it is found there only in an enlarged, transformed and idealized form. In this respect, the most primitive religions do not differ from the most recent and the most refined. For example, we have seen how the Arunta place at the

beginning of time a mythical society whose organization exactly reproduces that which still exists to-day; it includes the same clans and
phratries, it is under the same matrimonail rules and it practises the
same rites. But the personages who compose it are ideal beings, gifted
with powers and virtues to which common mortals cannot pretend.
Their nature is not only higher, but it is different, since it is at once
animal and human. The evil powers there undergo a similar meta-
morphosis: evil itself is, as it were, made sublime and idealized. The
question now raises itself of whence this idealization comes.

Some reply that men have a natural faculty for idealizing, that is to
say, of substituting for the real world another different one, to which
they transport themselves by thought. But that is merely changing the
terms of the problem; it is not resolving it or even advancing it. This
systematic idealization is an essential characteristic of religions. Explaining them by an innate power of idealization is simply replacing
one word by another which is the equivalent of the first; it is as if they
said that men have made religions because they have a religious nature.
Animals know only one world, the one which they perceive by experience, internal as well as external. Men alone have the faculty of
conceiving the ideal, of adding something to the real. Now where does
this singular privilege come from? Before making it an initial fact or
a mysterious virtue which escapes science, we must be sure that it does
not depend upon empirically determinable conditions.

The explanation of religion which we have proposed has precisely
this advantage, that it gives an answer to this question, For our definition of the sacred is that it is something added to and above the real:
now the ideal answers to this same definition; we cannot explain one
without explaining the other. In fact, we have seen that if collective
life awakens religious thought on reaching a certain degree of intensity,
it is because it brings about a state of effervescence which changes the
conditions of psychic activity. Vital energies are over-excited, passions
more active, sensations stronger. there are even some which are produced only at this moment. A man does not recognize himself; he feels
himself transformed and consequently he transforms the environment
which surrounds him. In order to account for the very particular impressions which he receives, he attributes to the things with which he
is in most direct contact properties which they have not, exceptional
powers and virtues which the objects of every-day experience do not
possess. In a word, above the real world where his profane life passes
he has placed another which, in one sense, does not exist except in
thought, but to which he attributes a higher sort of dignity than to the
first. Thus, from a double point of view it is an ideal world.

The formation of the ideal world is therefore not an irreducible fact which escapes science; it depends upon conditions which observation can touch; it is a natural product of social life. For a society to become conscious of itself and maintain at the necessary degree of intensity the sentiments which it thus attains, it must assemble and concentrate itself. No this concentration brings about an exaltation of the mental life which takes form in a group of ideal conceptions where it portrayed the new life thus awakened; they correspond to this new set of physical forces which is added to those which we have at our disposition for the daily tasks of existence. A society can neither create itself nor recreate itself without at the same time creating an ideal. This creation is not a sort of work of supererogation for it, by which it would complete itself, being already formed; it is the act by which it is periodically made and remade. Therefore when some oppose the ideal society to the real society, like two antagonists which would lead us in opposite directions, they materialize and oppose abstractions. The ideal society is not outside of the real society; it is a part of it. Far from being divided between them as between two poles which mutually repel each other, we cannot hold to one without holding to the other. For a society is not made up merely of the mass of individuals who compose it, the ground which they occupy, the things which they use and the movements which they perform, but above all is the idea which it forms of itself. It is undoubtedly true that it hesitates over the manner in which it ought to conceive itself; it feels itself drawn in divergent directions. But these conflicts which break forth are not between the ideal and reality, but between two different ideals, that of yesterday and that of to-day, that which has the authority of tradition and that which has the hope of the future. There is surely a place for investigating whence these ideals evolve; but whatever solution may be given to this problem, it still remains that all passes in the world of the ideal.

Thus the collective ideal which religion expresses is far from being due to a vague innate power of the individual, but it is rather at the school of collective life that the individual has learned to idealize. It is in assimilating the ideals elaborated by society that he has become capable of conceiving the ideal. It is society which, by leading him within its sphere of action, has made him acquire the need of raising himself above the world of experience and has at the same time furnished him with the means of conceiving another. For society has constructed this new world in constructing itself, since it is society which this expresses. Thus both with the individual and in the group, the faculty of idealizing has nothing mysterious about it. It is not a sort of luxury which a man could get along without, but the condition of his very existence. He could not be a social being, that is to say, he could not be a man, if he had not acquired it. It is true that in incarnating themselves in individuals, collective ideals tend to individualize themselves. Each understands them after his own fashion and marks them with his own stamp; he suppresses certain elements and adds others. Thus the personal ideal disengages itself from the society ideal in proportion as the individual personality develops itself and becomes an autonomous source of action. But if we wish to understand this aptitude, so singular in appearance, of living outside of reality, it is enough to connect it with the social conditions upon which it depends.

Therefore it is necessary to avoid seeing in this theory of religion a simple restatement of historical materialism: that would be misunderstanding our thought to an extreme degree. In showing that religion is something essentially social, we do not mean to say that it confines itself to translating into another language the material forms of society and its immediate vital necessities. It is true that we take it as evident that social life depends upon its material foundation and bears its mark, just as the mental life of an individual depends upon his nervous system and in fact his whole organism. But collective consciousness is something more than a mere epiphenomenon of its morphological basis, just as individual consciousness is something more than a simple efflorescence of the nervous system. In order that the former may appear, a synthesis *sui generis* of particular consciousnesses is required. Now this synthesis has the effect of disengaging a whole world of sentiments, ideas and images which, once born, obey laws all their own. They attract each other, repel each other, unite, divide themselves, and multiply, though these combinations are not commanded and necessitated by the condition of the underlying reality. The life thus brought into being even enjoys so great an independence that it sometimes indulges in manifestations with no purpose or utility of any sort, for the mere pleasure of affirming itself. We have shown that this is often precisely the case with ritual activity and mythological thought.

[. . .]

Thus there is something eternal in religion which is destined to survive all the particular symbols in which religious though has successively enveloped itself. There can be no society which does not feel the need of upholding and reaffirming at regular intervals the collective sentiments and the collective ideas which make its unity and its personality. Now this moral remaking cannot be achieved except by the means of reunions, assemblies and meetings where the individuals, being closely united to one another, reaffirm in common their common sentiments; hence come ceremonies which do not differ from regular religious ceremonies, either in their object, the reults which they produce, or the processes employed to attain these results. What essential difference is there between an assembly of Christians celebrating the principal dates of the life of Christ, or of Jews remembering the exodus from Egypt of the promulgation of the decalogue, and a reunion of citizens commemorating the promulgation of a new moral or legal system or some great event in the national life?

If we find a little difficulty to-day in imagining what these feasts and ceremonies of the future could consist in, it is because we are going through a stage of transition and moral mediocrity. [. . .]

But feasts and rites, in a word, the cult, are not the whole religion. This is not merely a system of practices, but also a system of ideas whose object is to explain the world; we have seen that even the humblest have their cosmology. Whatever connection there may be between these two elements of the religious life, they are still quite different. The one is turned towards action, which it demands and regulates; the other is turned towards thought, which it enriches and organizes. Then they do not depend upon the same conditions, and consequently it may be asked if the second answers to necessities as universal and as permanent as the first.

When specific characteristics are attributed to religious thought, and when it is believed that its function is to express, by means peculiar to itself, an aspect of reality which evades ordinary knowledge as well as science, one naturally refuses to admit that religion can ever abandon its speculative rôle. But our analysis of the facts does not seem to have shown this specific quality of religion. The religion which we have just studied is one of those whose symbols are the most disconcerting for this reason. There all appears mysterious. These beings which belong to the most heterogeneous groups at the same time, who multiply without ceasing to be one, who divide without diminishing, all seem, at first view, to belong to an entirely different world from the one where we live; some have even gone so far as to say that the mind which constructuted them ignored the laws of logic completely. Perhaps the contrast between reason and faith has never been more thorough. Then if there has ever been a moment in history when their heterogeneousness should have stood out clearly, it is here. But contrary to all appearances, as we have pointed out, the realities to which religious speculation is then applied are the same as those which later serve as the subject of reflection for philosophers: they are nature, man, society. The mystery which appears to surround them is wholly superficial and disappears before a more painstaking observation: it is enough merely to set aside the veil with which mythological imagination has covered them for them to appear such as they really are. Religion sets itself to translate these realities into an intelligible language which does not differ in nature from that employed by science; the attempt is made by both to connect things with each other, to establish internal relations between them, to classify them and to systematize them. We have seen that the essential ideas of scientific logic are of religious origin. It is true that in order to utilize them, science gives them a new elaboration; it purges theme of all accidental elements; in a general way, it brings a spirit of criticism into all its doings, which religion ignores; it surrounds itself with precautions to 'escape precipitation and bias,' and to hold aside the passions, prejudices and all subjective influences. But these perfectionings of method are not enough to differentiate it from religion. In this regard, both pursue the same end; scientific thought is only a more perfect form of religious thought. Thus it seems natural that the second should progressively retire before the first, as this becomes better fitted to perform the task.

And there is no doubt that this regression has taken place in the course of history. Having left religion, science tends to substitute itself for this latter in all that which concerns the cognitive and intellectual functions. Christianity has already definitely consecrated this substitution in the order of material things. Seeing in matter that which is profane before all else, it readily left the knowledge of this to another discipline, *tradidit mundum hominum disputationi,* 'He gave the world over to the disputes of men'; it is thus that the natural sciences have been able to establish themselves and make their authority recognized without very great difficulty. But it could not give up the world of souls so easily; for it is before all over souls that the god of the Christians aspires to reign. That is why the idea of submitting the psychic life to science produced the effect of a sort of profanation for a long time; even to-day it is repugnant to many minds. However, experimental and comparative psychology is founded and to-day we must reckon with it. the world of the religious and moral life is still forbidden. The great majority of men continue to believe that here there is an order of things which the mind cannot penetrate except by very special ways. Hence comes the active resistance which is met with every time that someone tries to treat religious and moral phenomena scientifically. But in spite of these oppositions, these attempts are constantly repeated and this persistence even allows us to foresee that this final barrier will finally give way and that science will establish herself as mistress even in this reserved region.

That is what the conflict between science and religion really amounts to. It is said that science denies religion in principle. But religion exists; it is a system of given facts; in a word, it is a reality. How could science deny this reality? Also, in so far as religion is action, and in so far as it is a means of making men live, science could not take its place, for even if this expresses life, it does not create it; it may well seek to explain the faith, but by that very act it presupposes it. Thus there is no conflict except upon one limited point. Of the two functions which religion originally fulfilled, there is one, and only one, which tends to escape it more and more: that is its speculative function. That which science refuses to grant to religion is not its right to exist, but its right to dogmatize upon the nature of things and the special competence which it claims for itself for knowing man and the world. As a matter of fact, it does not know itself. It does not even know what it is made of, nor to what need it answers. It is itself a subject for science, so far is it from being able to make the law for science! And from another point of view, since there is no proper subject for religious speculation outside that reality to which scientific reflection is applied, it is evident that this former cannot play the same rôle in the future that it has played in the past.

However, it seems destined to transform itself rather than to disappear.

We have said that there is something eternal in religion: it is the cult and the faith. Men cannot celebrate ceremonies for which they see no reason, nor can they accept a faith which they in no way understand. To spread itself or merely to maintain itself, it must be justified, that is to say, a theory must be made of it. A theory of this sort must undoubtedly be founded upon the different sciences, from the moment when these exist; first of all, upon the social sciences, for religious faith has its origin in society; then upon psychology, for society is a synthesis of human consciousnesses; and finally upon the sciences of nature, for man and society are a part of the universe and can be abstracted from it only artificially. But howsoever important these facts taken from the constituted sciences may be, they are not enough; for faith is before all else an impetus to action, while science, no matter how far it may be pushed, always remains at a distance from this. Science is fragmentary and incomplete; it advances but slowly and is never finished; but life cannot wait. The theories which are destined to make men live and act are therefore obliged to pass science and complete it prematurely. They are possible only when the practical exigencies and the vital necessities which we feel without distinctly conceiving them push thought in advance, beyond that which science permits us to affirm. Thus religions, even the most rational and laicized, cannot and never will be able to dispense with a particular form of speculation which, though having the same subjects as science itself, cannot be really scientific: the obscure intuitions of sensation and sentiment too often take the place of logical reasons. On one side, this speculation resembles that which we meet with in the religions of the past; but on another, it is different. While claiming and exercising the right of going beyond science, it must commence by knowing this and by inspiring itself with it. Ever since the authority of science was established, it must be reckoned with; one can go farther than it under the pressure of necessity, but he must take his direction from it. He can affirm nothing that it denies, deny nothing that it affirms, and establish nothing that is not directly or indirectly founded upon principles taken from it. From now on, the faith no longer exercises the same hegemony as formerly over the system of ideas that we my continue to call religion. A rival power rises up before it which, being born of it, ever after submits it to its criticism and control. And everything makes us foresee that this control will constantly become more extended and efficient, while no limit can be assigned to its future influence.

Reading 8

PRIMITIVE CLASSIFICATION

Primitive classifications are therefore not singular or exceptional, having no analogy with those employed by more civilized peoples; on the contrary, they seem to be connected, with no break in continuity, to the first scientific classifications. In fact, however different they may be in certain respects from the latter, they nevertheless have all their essential characteristics. First of all, like all sophisticated classifications, they are systems of hierarchical notions. Things are not simply arranged by them in the form of isolated groups, but these groups stand in fixed relationships to each other and together form a single whole. Moreover, these systems, like those of science, have a purely speculative purpose. Their object is not to facilitate action, but to advance understanding, to make intelligible the relations which exist between things. Given certain concepts which are considered to be fundamental, the mind feels the need to connect to them the ideas which it forms about other things. Such classifications are thus intended, above all, to connect ideas, to unify knowledge; as such, they

Edited and reprinted with premission from: E. Durkheim and M. Mauss, *Primitive Classification*, translated by R. Needham, London, Cohen & West, 1963, pp. 81–4. Originally published as 'De quelques formes primitives de classification', *Année Sociologique*, 1901–2 (1903).

may be said without inexactitude to be scientific, and to constitute a first philosophy of nature.[1] The Australian does not divide the universe between the totems of his tribe with a view to regulating his conduct or even to justify his practice; it is because, the idea of the totem being cardinal for him, he is under a necessity to place everything else that he knows in relation to it. We may therefore think that the conditions on which these very ancient classifications depend may have played an important part in the genesis of the classificatory function in general.

Now it results from this study that the nature of these conditions is social. Far from it being the case, as Frazer seems to think, that the social relations of men are based on logical relations between things, in reality it is the former which have provided the prototype for the latter. According to him, men were divided into clans by a pre-existing classification of things; but, quite on the contrary, they classified things because they were divided by clans.

We have seen, indeed, how these classifications were modelled on the closest and most fundamental form of social organization. This, however, is not going far enough. Society was not simply a model which classificatory thought followed; it was its own divisions which served as divisions for the system of classification. The first logical categories were social categories; the first classes of things were classes of men, into which these things were integrated. It was because men were grouped, and thought of themselves in the form of groups, that in their ideas they grouped other things, and in the beginning the two modes of grouping were merged to the point of being indistinct. Moieties were the first genera; clans, the first species. Things were thought to be integral parts of society, and it was their place in society which determined their place in nature. We may even wonder whether the schematic manner in which genera are ordinarily conceived may not have depended in part on the same influences. It is a fact of current observation that the things which they comprise are generally imagined as situated in a sort of ideational milieu, with a more or less clearly delimited spatial

[1] As such they are clearly distinguished from what might be called technological classifications. It is probable that man has always classified, more or less clearly, the things on which he lived, according to the means he used to get them: for example, animals living in the water, or in the air or on the ground. But at first such groups were not connected with each other or systematized. They were divisions, distinctions of ideas, not schemes of classification. Moreover, it is evident that these distinctions are closely linked to practical concerns, of which they merely express certain aspects. It is for this reason that we have not spoken of them in this work, in which we have tried above all to throw some light on the origins of the logical procedure which is the basis of scientific classifications.

circumscription. It is certainly not without cause that concepts and their interrelations have so often been represented by concentric and eccentric circles, interior and exterior to each other, etc. Might it not be that this tendency to imagine purely logical groupings in a form contrasting so much with their true nature originated in the fact that at first they were conceived in the form of social groups occupying, consequently, definite positions in space? And have we not in fact seen this spatial localization of genus and species in a fairly large number of very different societies.

Not only the external form of classes, but also the relations uniting them to each other, are of social origin. It is because human groups fit one into another — the sub-clan into the clan, the clan into the moiety, the moiety into the tribe — that groups of things are ordered in the same way. Their regular diminution in span, from genus to species, species to variety, and so on, comes from the equally diminishing extent presented by social groups as one leaves the largest and oldest and approaches the more recent and the more derivative. And if the totality of things is conceived as a single system, this is because society itself is seen in the same way. It is a whole, or rather it is *the* unique whole to which everything is related. Thus logical hierarchy is only another aspect of social hierarchy, and the unity of knowledge is nothing else than the very unity of the collectivity, extended to the universe.

Part Six

Politics

Reading 9

PROFESSIONAL ETHICS AND CIVIC MORALS

PROFESSIONAL ETHICS

If we were to attempt to fix in definite language the ideas current on
what the relations should be of the employee with his chief, of the
workman with the manager, of the rival manufacturers with each other
and with the public — what vague and equivocal formulas we should
get! Some hazy generalizations on the loyalty and devotion owed by
staff and workmen to those employing them; some phrases on the
moderation the employer should use in his economic dominance; some
reproach for any too overtly unfair competition — that is about all
there is in the moral consciousness of the various professions we are
discussing. Injunctions as vague and as far removed from the facts as
these could not have any very great effect on conduct. Moreover,
there is nowhere any organ with the duty of seeing they are enforced.
They have no sanctions other than those which a diffused public
opinion has at hand, and since that opinion is not kept lively by frequent contact between individuals and since it therefore cannot exer-

From: *Professional Ethics and Civil Morals*, translated by C. Brookfield, London,
Routledge & Kegan Paul, 1957, pp. 9–13, 28–40,42–51, 61–64, 69–73, 211–
218. From the French *Leçons de Sociologie*, Turkey, University of Istanbul,
1950.

cise enough control over individual actions, it is lacking both in stability and authority. The result is that professional ethics weigh very lightly on the consciousnesses and are reduced to something so slight that they might as well not be. Thus, there exists to-day a whole range of collective activity outside the sphere of morals and which is almost entirely removed from the moderating effect of obligations.

Is this state of affairs a normal one? It has had the support of famous doctrines. To start with, there is the classical economic theory according to which the free play of economic agreements should adjust itself and reach stability automatically, without its being necessary or even possible to submit it to any restraining forces. This, in a sense, underlies most of the Socialist doctrines. Socialist theory, in fact, like classical economic theory holds that economic life is equipped to organize itself and to function in an orderly way and in harmony, without any moral authority intervening; this, however, depends on a radical change in the laws of property, so that things cease to be in the exclusive ownership of individuals or families and instead, are transferred to the hands of the society. Once this were done, the State would do no more than keep accurate statistics of the wealth produced over given periods and distribute this wealth amongst the associate members according to an agreed formula. Now, both these theories do no more than raise a *de facto* state of affairs which is unhealthy, to the level of a *de jure* state of affairs. It is true, indeed, that economic life has this character at the present day, but it is impossible for it to preserve this, even at the price of a thoroughgoing change in the structure of property. It is not possible for a social function to exist without moral discipline. Otherwise, nothing remains but individual appetites, and since they are by nature boundless and insatiable, if there is nothing to control them they will not be able to control themselves.

And it is precisely due to this fact that the crisis has arisen from which the European societies are now suffering. For two centuries economic life has taken on an expansion it never knew before. From being a secondary function, despised and left to inferior classes, it passed on to one of first rank. We see the military, governmental and religious functions falling back more and more in face of it. The scientific functions alone are in a position to dispute its ground, and even science has hardly any prestige in the eyes of the present day, except in so far as it may serve what is materially useful, that is to say, serve for the most part the business professions. There has been talk, and not without reason, of societies becoming mainly industrial. A form of activity that promises to occupy such a place in society taken as a whole cannot be exempt from all precise moral regulation, without a state of anarchy ensuing. The forces thus released can have no guidance for their normal development, since there is nothing to point out where a halt should be called. There is a head-on clash when the moves of rivals conflict, as they attempt to encroach on another's field or to beat him down or drive him out. Certainly the stronger succeed in crushing the not so strong or at any rate in reducing them to a state of subjection. But since this subjection is only a *de facto* condition sanctioned by no kind of morals, it is accepted only under duress until the longed-for day of revenge. Peace treaties signed in this fashion are always provisional, forms of truce that do not mean peace to men's minds. This is how these ever-recurring conflicts arise between the different factions of the economic structure. If we put forward this anarchic competition as an ideal we should adhere to — one that should even be put into practice more radically than it is to-day — then we should be confusing sickness with a condition of good health. On the other hand, we shall not get away from this simply by modifying once and for all the lay-out of economic life; for whatever we contrive, whatever new arrangements be introduced, it will still not become other than it is or change its nature. By its very nature, it cannot be self-sufficing. A state of order or peace amongst men cannot follow of itself from any entirely material causes, from any blind mechanism, however scientific it may be. It is a moral task.

From yet another point of view, this amoral character of economic life amounts to a public danger. The functions of this order to-day absorb the energies of the greater part of the nation. The lives of a host of individuals are passed in the industrial and commercial sphere. Hence, it follows that, as those in this *milieu* have only a faint impress of morality, the greater part of their existence is passed divorced from any moral influence. How could such a state of affairs fail to be a source of demoralization? If a sense of duty is to take strong root in us, the very circumstances of our life must serve to keep it always active. There must be a group about us to call it to mind all the time and, as often happens, when we are tempted to turn a deaf ear. A way of behaviour, no matter what it be, is set on a steady course only through habit and exercise. If we live amorally for a good part of the day, how can we keep the springs of morality from going slack in us? We are not naturally inclined to put ourselves out or to use self-restraint; if we are not encouraged at every step to exercise the restraint upon which all morals depend, how should we get the habit of it? If we follow no rule except that of a clear self-interest, in the occupations that take up nearly the whole of our time, how should we acquire a taste for any disinterestedness, or selflessness or sacrifice? Let us see, then, how the unleashing of economic interests has been accompanied by a debasing of public morality. We find that the manufacturer, the merchant, the workman, the employee, in carrying on his occupation is aware of no influence set above them to check his egotism; he is subject to no moral discipline whatever and so he scouts any discipline at all of this kind.

It is therefore extremely important that economic life should be regulated, should have its moral standards raised, so that the conflicts that disturb it have an end, and further, that individuals should cease to live thus within a moral vacuum where the life-blood drains away even from individual morality. For in this order of social functions there is need for professional ethics to be established, nearer the concrete, closer to the facts, with a wider scope than anything existing to-day. There should be rules telling each of the workers his rights and his duties, not vaguely in general terms but in precise detail, having in view the most ordinary day-to-day occurrences. All these various interrelations cannot remain for ever in a state of fluctuating balance. A system of ethics, however is not to be improvised. It is the task of the very group to which they are to apply. When they fail, it is because the cohesion of the group is at fault, because as a group its existence is too shadowy and the rudimentary state of its ethics goes to show its lack of imagination. Therefore, the true cure for the evil is to give the professional groups in the economic order a stability they so far do not possess. Whilst the craft union or corporate body is nowadays only a collection of individuals who have no lasting ties with one another, it must become or return to being a well-defined and organized association. Any notion of this kind, however, comes up against historical prejudices that make it still repugnant to most, and on that account it is necessary to dispel them.

[. . .]

Besides the historic prejudice we spoke of last time, there is a further fact that has led to the guild system being discredited: it is the revulsion that is generally aroused by the idea of economic control by rule. In our own minds we see all regulation of this sort as a kind of policing, maybe vexatious, maybe endurable, and possibly calling forth some outward reaction from individuals, but making no appeal to the mind and without any root in the consciousness. It appears like some vast set of workshop regulations, far-reaching and framed in general terms: those who have to submit to them may obey in practice if they must, but they could not really want to have them. Thus, the discipline laid down by an individual and imposed by him in military fashion on other individuals who in point of fact are not concerned in wanting them, is confused by us with a collective discipline to which the members of a group are committed. Such discipline can only be maintained if it rests on a state of public opinion and has its roots in morals, it is these morals that count. An established control by rule does no more, shall we say, than define them with greater precision and give them sanction. It tranlates into precepts ideas and sentiments felt by all, that is, a common adherence to the same objective.

[. . .]

It is only through the corporative system that the moral standard of economic life can be raised. We can give some idea of the present situation by saying that the greater part of the social functions (and this greater part means to-day the economic – so wide is their range) are almost devoid of any moral influence, at any rate in what is their own field. To be sure, the rules of common morality apply to them, but they are rules made for a life in common and not for this specific kind of life. Further, they are rules governing those relations of the specific kind of life which are not peculiar to industry and commerce: they do not apply to the others. And why, indeed, in the case of those others, should there be no need to submit to a moral influence? What is to become of public morality if there is so little trace of the principle of duty in this whole sphere that is so important in the social life? There are professional ethics for the priest, the soldier, the lawyer, the magistrate, and so on. Why should there not be one for trade and industry? Why should there not be obligations of the employee towards the employer and vice versa; or of business men one towards the other, so as to lessen or regulate the competition they set up and to prevent it from turning into a conflict sometimes – as to-day – almost as cruel as actual warfare? All these rights and obligations cannot, however, be the same in all branches of industry: they have to vary according to the conditions in each. The obligations in the agricultural industry are not those obtaining in the unhealthy industries, nor of course do those in commerce correspond to those in what we call industry, and so on. A comparison may serve to let us realize where we stand on these points. In the human body all visceral functions are controlled by a particular part of the nervous system other than the brain: this consists of the sympathetic nerve and the vagus or pneumogastric nerves. Well, in our society, too, there is a brain which controls the function of inter-relationship; but the visceral functions, the functions of the vegetative life or what corresponds to them, are subject to no regulative action. Let us imagine what would happen to the functions of hearts, lungs, stomach and so on, if they were free like this of all discipline. . . . Just such a spectacle is presented by nations where there are no regulative organs of economic life. To be sure, the social brain, that is, the State, tries hard to take their place and carry out their functions. But it is unfitted for it and its intervention, when not simply powerless, causes troubles of another kind.

That is why I believe that no reform has greater urgency. I will not say it would achieve everything, but it is the preliminary condition that makes all the others possible. Let us suppose that by a miracle the whole system of property is entirely transformed overnight and that on the collectivist formula the means of production are taken out of the hands of individuals and made over absolutely to collective ownership. All the problems around us that we are debating to-day will still persist in their entirety. There will always be an economic mechanism and various agencies to combine in making it work. The rights and obligations of these various agencies therefore have to be determined and in the different branches of industry at that. So a corpus of rules has to be laid down, fixing the stint of work, the pay of the members of staff and their obligations to one another, towards the community, and so on. This means, then, that we should still be faced with a blank page to work on. Supposing the means – the machinery of labour – had been taken out of these hands or those and placed in others, we should still not know how the machinery worked or what the economic life should be, nor what to do in the face of this change in conditions. The state of anarchy would still persist; for, let me repeat, this state of anarchy comes about not from this machinery being in these hands and not in those, but because the activity deriving from it is not regulated. And it will not be regulated, nor its moral standard raised, by any witchcraft. This control by rule and raising of moral standards can be established neither by the scientist in his study nor by the statesman; it has to be the task of the groups concerned. Since these groups do not exist at the present time, it is of the greatest urgency that they be created. The other problems can only be usefully tackled after that.

[. . .]

Let us imagine – spread over the whole country – the various industries grouped in separate categories based on similarity and natural affinity. An adminstrative council, a kind of miniature parliament, nominated by election, would preside over each group. We go on to imagine this council or parliament as having the power, on a scale to be fixed, to regulate whatever concerns the business: relations of employers and employed – conditions of labour – wages and salaries – relations of competitors one with another, and so on . . . and there we have the guild restored, but in an entirely novel form. The establishment of this central organ appointed for the management of the group in general, would in no way exclude the forming of subsidiary and regional organs under its direction and subordinate to it. The general rules to be laid down by it might be made specific and adapted to apply to various parts of the area by industrial boards. These would be more regional in character just as to-day under Parliament there are councils for the *département* or municipality. In this way, economic life would be organized, regulated and defined, without losing any of its diversity. Such organization would do no more than introduce into the economic order the reforms already made in all other spheres of the national life. Customs, morals, political administration, all of which formerly had a local character and varied from place to place, have gradually moved towards uniformity and to a loss of diversity. The former autonomous organs, the tribunals, the feudal and communal powers, have become with time auxiliary organs, subordinate to the central organism that took shape. Is it not to be expected that the economic order will be transformed with the same trend and by the same process? What existed at the outset was a local structure, an affair of the community: what has to take its place is not a complete absence of organization, a state of anarchy; rather it would be a structure that was comprehensive and national, uniform and at the same time complex, in which the local groupings of the past would still survive, but simply as agencies to ensure communication and diversity. [. . .]

This seems to be the fundamental principle of the only kind of corporative system that would be appropriate to large-scale industry. We have shown the outlines, and it remains to solve a number of secondary questions that cannot be dealt with here. I shall only touch on the most important.

To begin with, it is often asked whether the guild should be compulsory, whether or no individuals should be bound to membership. This question, I feel, is only of limited interest. In fact, from the day when the guild system was set up, it would be such a handicap for the individual to remain aloof the he would join of his own accord, without any need of coercion. Once constituted, a collective force draws into its orbit those who are unattached: any who remain outside are unable to hold their ground. Moreover, it is beyond me to understand the scruples that some feel in this case against any suggestion of compulsion. Every citizen nowadays is obliged to be attached to a *commune* (parish). Why then should the same principle not apply to the profession or calling? All the more, since in fact the reform we are discussing would in the end result in the professional association taking the place of the jurisdictional areas as a political unit of the region.

A more important matter is to know what the respective place and part of employer and employed would be in the corporative structure. It seems to me obvious that both should be represented in the governing body responsible for supervising the general affairs and well-being of the association. Such a body could only carry out its function provided that it included both these elements. However, one is forced to wonder whether a distinction would not have to be made at the base of the structure: whether the two categories of industrial personnel would not have to nominate their representatives separately — in a word, whether the electoral bodies would not have to be independent, at all events when their respective interests were obviously in conflict.

Finally, it seems certain that this whole framework should be attached to the central organ, that is, to the State. Occupational legislation could hardly be other than an application in particular of the law in general, just as professional ethics can only be a special form of common morality. To be sure, there will always be all the various forms of economic activity of individuals, which involve such overall regulation, and this cannot be the task of any group in particular.

So far, we have only briefly indicated the functions which might take shape in the corporative body. We cannot foresee all those which might be assigned to it in the future. Our best course is to keep to those which could be handed over to it straight away. From the legislative point of view, certain functions have to be classified according to the industry, such as the general principles of the labour contract, of salary and wages remuneration, of industrial health, of all that concerns the labour of women and children, etc., and the State is incapable of such classification. The provision of superannuation and provident funds, etc. cannot be made over without danger to the funds of the State, overburdened as it is with various services, as well as being too far removed from the individual. Finally, the regulation of labour disputes, which cannot be codified as laws on any hard and fast principle, calls for special tribunals. In order to adjudicate with entire independence, these would have rights that varied with the varying forms of industry. There we have the judicial task, which might be assigned henceforth to the guilds in their revived and altered form. [. . .]

DEFINITION OF THE STATE

An essential element that enters into the notion of any political group is the opposition between governing and governed, between authority and those subject to it. It is quite possible that in the beginning of social evolution this gap may not have existed; such an hypothesis is all the more likely since we do find societies in which the distance between the two is only faintly perceptible. But in any case, the societies where it is seen cannot be mistaken for those where it does not occur. The former differ from the latter in kind and require different terms of description: we should keep the word 'political' for the first category. For if this expression has any one meaning, it is, above all, organization, at any rate rudimentary; it is established authority (whether stable or intermittent, weak or strong), to whose action individuals are subject, whatever it be.

But an authority of this type is not found solely in political societies. The family has a head whose powers are sometimes limited by those of a family council. The patriarchal family of the Romans has often been compared to a State in miniature. Although, as we shall soon see, this expression is not justified, we could not quarrel with it if the sole distinguishing feature of the political society were a governmental structure. So we must look for some further characteristic.

This lies possibly in the especially close ties that bind any political society to its soil. There is said to be an enduring relationship between any nation and a given territory. "The State", says Bluntschli, "must have its domain; the nation demands a country." But the family, at least in many countries, is no less bound to the soil — that is, to some charted area. The family, too, has its domain from which it is inseparable, since that domain is inalienable. We have seen that the patrimony of landed estate was sometimes the very kernel of the family; it is this patrimony that made its unity and continuity and it was about this focus that domestic life revolved. Nowhere, in any political society, has political territory had a status to compare with this in importance. We may add, however, that were cardinal importance attaches to national territory, it is of comparatively recent date. To begin with, it seems rater arbitrary to deny any political character to the great nomad societies whose structure was sometimes very elaborate. Again, in the past it was the number of citizens and not the territory that was considered to be the primary element of the State. To annex a State was not to annex the country but its inhabitants and to incorporate them within the annexing State. On the other hand, we may see the victors preparing to settle down in the country vanquished, without thereby losing their own cohesion or their political identity. During the whole early period of our history, the capital, that is, the territorial centre of gravity of the society, had an extreme mobility. It is not a great while since the peoples became so identified with the territories they inhabit, that is, with what we should call the geographical expression of those peoples. To-day, France is not only a mass of people consisting in the main of individuals speaking a certain language and who observe certain laws and so on, but essentially a certain defined part of Europe. If indeed all the Alsatians had opted for French nationality in 1870, we might have with justice still considered France as mutilated or diminished, by the sole fact that she had abandoned a delimited part of her soil to a foreign Power. But this identification of the society with its territory has only come about in those societies that are the most advanced. To be sure, it is due to many causes, to the higher social value that the soil has gained, perhaps also to the relatively greater importance that the geographical bond has assumed since other social ties of a more moral kind have lost their force. The society of which we are members is in our minds all the more a well-defined territory, since it is no longer in its essence a religion, a corpus of traditions peculiar to it or the cult of a particular dynasty.

Leaving territory aside, should we not find a feature of a political society in the numerical importance of the population? It is true we should not ordinarily give this name to social groups comprising a very small number of individuals. Even so, a dividing line of this kind would be extremely fluctuating: for at what precise moment does a concentration of people become of a size to be classified as a political group? [. . .]

Nevertheless, we touch here on a distinctive feature. To be sure, we cannot say that a political society differs from family groups or from professional groups on the score that it has greater numbers, for the numerical strength of families may in some instances be considerable while the numerical strength of a State may be very small. But it remains true that there is no political society which does not compromise numerous different families of professional groups or both at once. If it were confined to a domestic society or family, it would be identical with it and hence be a domestic society. But the moment it is made up of a certain number of domestic societies, the resulting aggregate is something other than each of its elements. It is something new, which has to be described by a different word. Likewise, the political society cannot be identified with any professional group or with any caste, if caste there be; but is always an aggregate of various professions or various castes, as it is of different families. More often, when we get a society made up of a collection of secondary groups varying in kind, without itself being a secondary group in relation to a far bigger society, then it constitutes a social entity of a specific kind. We should then define the political society as one formed by the coming together of a rather large number of secondary social groups, subject to the same one authority which is not itself subject to any other authority duly constituted.

[. . .]

Now that we know the distinguishing marks of a political society, let us see what the morals are that relate to it. From the very definition just made, it follows that the essential rules of these morals are those determining the relation of individuals to this sovereign authority, to whose control they are subject. Since we need a word to indicate the particular group of officials entrusted with representing this authority, we are agreed to keep for this purpose the word 'State'. It is true that very often we apply the word State not to the instrument of government but to the political society as a whole, or to the people governed and its government taken as one, and we ourselves often use the term in this sense. It is in this way that we speak of the European States or that we call France a State. But since it is well to have separate terms for existent things as different as the society and one of its organs, we apply the term 'State' more especially to the agents of the sovereign authority, and 'political society' to the complex group of which the State is the highest organ. This being granted, the principal duties under civic morals are obviously those the citizen has towards the State and, conversely, those the State owes to the individual. To understand what these duties are, we must first of all determine the nature and function of the State.

It is true it may seem that we have already answered the first question and that the nature of the State has been defined at the same time as the political society. Is not the State the supreme authority to which the political society as a whole is subordinate? But in fact this term authority is pretty vague and needs definition. Where does the group of officials vested with this authority begin and end, and who constitute, properly speaking, the State? The question is all the more called for, since current speech creates more confusion on the subject. Every day, we hear the public services are State services; the Law, the army, the Church — where there is a national Church — are held to form part of the State. But we must not confuse with the State itself the secondary organs in the immediate field of its control, which in relation to it are only executive. At very least, the groups or special groups (for the State is complex) — to which these secondary groups (called more specifically administrative) are subordinate, must be distinguished from the State. The characteristic feature of the special groups is that they alone are entitled to think and to act instead of representing the society. The representations,[1] like the solutions that are

[1] NB. in E.D.'s sense of word.

worked out in this special *milieu* are inherently and of necessity collective. It is true, there are many representations and many collective decisions beyond those that take shape in this way. In every society there are or have been myths and dogmas, whenever the political society and the Church are one and the same, as well as historical and moral traditions: these make the representations common to all members of the society but are not in the special province of any one particular organ. There exist too at all times social currents wholly unconnected with the State, that draw the collectivity in this or that direction. Frequently it is a case of the State coming under their pressure, rather than itself giving the impulse to them. In this way a whole psychic life is diffused throughout the society. But it is a different one that has a fixed existence in the organ of government. It is here that this other psychic life develops and when in time it begins to have its effect on the rest of the society, it is only in a minor way and by repercussions. When a bill is carried in Parliament, when the government takes a decision within the limits of its competence, both actions, it is true, depend on the general state of social opinion, and on the society. Parliament and the government are in touch with the mass of the nation and the various impressions released by this contact have their effect in deciding them to take this course rather than that. But even if there be this one factor in their decision lying outside themselves, it is none the less true that it is they (Parliament and government) who make this decision and above all it expresses the particular *milieu* where it has its origin. It often happens, too, that there may even be discord between this *milieu* and the nation as a whole, and that decisions taken by the government or parliamentary vote may be valid for the whole community and yet do not square with the state of social opinion. So we may say that there is a collective psychic life, but this life is not diffused throughout the entire social body: although collective, it is localised in a specific organ. And this localisation does not come about simply through concentration on a given point of a life having its origins outside this point. It is in part at this very point that it has its beginning. When the State takes thought and makes a decision, we must not say that it is the society that thinks and decides through the State, but that the State thinks and decides for it. It is not simply an instrument for canalizing and concentrating. It is, in a certain sense, the organizing centre of the secondary groups themselves.

Let us see how the State can be defined. It is a group of officials *sui generis,* within which representations and acts of volition involving the collectivity are worked out, although they are not the product of collectivity. It is not accurate to say that the State embodies the collective consciousness, for that goes beyond the State at every point. In the main, that consciousness is diffused: there is at all times a vast number of social sentiments and social states of mind (*états*) of all kinds, of which the State hears only a faint echo. The State is the centre only of a particular kind of consciousness, of one that is limited but higher, clearer and with a more vivid sense of itself. There is nothing so obscure and so indefinite as these collective representations that are spread throughout all societies — myths, religious or moral legends, and so on. . . . We do not know whence they come nor whither they are tending; we have never had them under examination. The representations that derive from the State are always more conscious of themselves, of their causes and their aims. These have been concerted in a way that is less obscured. The collective agency which plans them realizes better what it is about. There too, it is true, there is often a good deal of obscurity. The State, like the individual, is often mistaken as to the motives underlying its decisions, but whether its decisions be ill motivated or not, the main thing is that they should be motivated to some extent. There is always or at least usually a semblance of deliberation, an understanding of the circumstances as a whole that make the decision necessary, and it is precisely this inner organ of the State that is called upon to conduct these debates. Hence, we have these councils, these regulations, these assemblies, these debates that make it impossible for these kinds of representation to evolve except at a slow pace. To sum up, we can therefore say that the State is a special organ whose responsibility it is to work out certain representations which hold good for the collectivity. These representations are distinguished from the other collective representations by their higher degree of consciousness and reflection.

We may perhaps feel some surprise at finding excluded from this definition all idea of action or execution or achievement of plans outside the State. Is it not generally held that this part of the State (at all events the part more precisely called the government), has the executive power? This view, however, is altogether out of place: the State does not execute anything. The Council of ministers or the sovereign do not themselves take action any more than Parliament: they give the orders for action to be taken. They co-ordinate ideas and sentiments, from these they frame decisions and transmit these decisions to other agencies that carry them out: but that is the limit of their office. In this respect there is no difference between Parliament (or the deliberative assemblies of all kinds surrounding the sovereign or head of State) and the government in the exact meaning of the term, the power known as executive. This power is called executive because it is closest to the executive agencies, but it is not to be identified with them. The whole life of the State, in its true meaning, consists not in exterior action, in making changes, but in deliberation, that is, in representations, the administrative bodies of all kinds, who are in charge of carrying out the changes. The difference between them and the State is clear: this difference is parallel to that between the muscular system and the central nervous system. Strictly speaking, the State is the very organ of social thought. As things are, this thought is directed towards an aim that is practical, not speculative. The State, as a rule at least, does not think for the sake of thought or to build up doctrinal systems, but to guide collective conduct. None the less, its principal function is to think.

[. . .]

RELATION OF THE STATE AND THE INDIVIDUAL

Every society is despotic, at least if nothing from without supervenes to restrain its despotism. Still, I would not say that there is anything artificial in this despotism: it is natural because it is necessary, and also because, in certain conditions, societies cannot endure without it. Nor do I mean that there is anything intolerable about it: on the contrary, the individual does not feel it any more than we feel the atmosphere that weighs on our shoulders. From the moment the individual has been raised in this way by the collectivity, he will naturally desire what it desires and accept without difficulty the state of subjection to which he finds himself reduced. If he is to be conscious of this and to resist it, individualist aspirations must find an outlet, and that they cannot do in these conditions.

But for it to be otherwise, we may say, would it not be enough for the society to be on a fairly large scale? There is no doubt that when it is small — when it surrounds every individual on all sides and at every moment — it does not allow of his evolving in freedom. If it be always present and always in action, it leaves no room to his initiative. But it is no longer in the same case when it has reached wide enough dimensions. When it is made up of a vast number of individuals, a society can exercise over each a supervision only as close and as vigilant and effective as when the surveillance is concentrated on a small number. A man is far more free in the midst of a throng than in a small coterie. Hence it follows that individual diversities can then more easily have play, that collective tyranny declines and that individualism establishes itself in fact, and that, with time, the fact becomes a right. Things can, however, only have this course on one condition: that is, that inside this society, there must be no forming of any secondary groups that enjoy enough autonomy to allow of each becoming in a way a small society within the greater. For then, each of these would behave towards its members as if it stood alone and everything would go on as if the full-scale society did not exist. Each group, tightly enclosing the individuals of which it was made up, would hinder their development; the collective mind would impose itself on conditions applying to the individual. [. . .]

Let us see why and how the main function of the State is to liberate the individual personalities. It is solely because, in holding its constituent societies in check, it prevents them from exerting the repressive influences over the individual that they would otherwise exert. So there is nothing inherently tyrannical about State intervention in the different fields of collective life; on the contrary, it has the object and the effect of alleviating tyrannies that do exist. It will be argued, might not the State in turn become despotic? Undoubtedly, provided there were nothing to counter that trend. In that case, as the sole existing collective force, it produces the effects that any collective force not neutralized by any counter-force of the same kind would have on individuals. The State itself then becomes a leveller and repressive. And its repressiveness becomes even harder to endure than that of small groups, because it is more artificial. The State, in our large-scale societies, is so removed from individual interests that it cannot take into account the special or local and other conditions in which they exist. Therefore when it does attempt to regulate them, it succeeds only at the cost of doing violence to them and distorting them. It is, too, not sufficiently in touch with individuals in the mass to be able to mould them inwardly, so that they readily accept its pressure on them. The individual eludes the State to some extent — the State can only be effective in the context of a large-scale society — and individual diversity may not come to light. Hence, all kinds of resistance and distressing conflicts arise. The small groups do not have this drawback. They are close enough to the things that provide their *raison d'être* to be able to adapt their actions exactly and they surround the individuals closely enough to shape them in their own image. The inference to be drawn from this comment, however, is simply that if that collective force, the State, is to be the liberator of the individual, it has itself need for some counter-balance; it must be restraind by other collective forces, that is, by those secondary groups we shall discuss later on. . . . It is not a good thing for the groups to stand alone, nevertheless they have to exist. And it is out of this conflict of social forces that individual liberties are born. Here again we see the significance of these groups. Their usefulness is not merely to regulate and govern the interests they are meant to serve. They have a wider purpose; they form one of the conditions essential to the emancipation of the individual.

It remains a fact that the State is not of its own volition antagonistic to the individual. It is only through the State that individualism is possible, although it cannot be the means of making it a reality, except in certain precise conditions. We might say that in the State we have the prime mover. It is the State that has rescued the child from patriarchal domination and from family tyranny; it is the State that has freed the citizen from feudal groups and later from communal groups; it is the State that has liberated the craftsman and his master from guild tyranny. It may take too violent a course, but the action becomes vitiated only when it is merely destructive. And that is what justifies the increasing scope of its functions. This concept of the State is, then, an individualistic one, but it does not limit the State to the administration of an entirely prohibitive justice. And in this concept there is recognition of the right and duty of the State to play the widest possible part in all that touches collective life, without however having a *mystique*.[2] For the purpose assigned to the State in this concept is comprehensible to individuals, just as they understand the links between the State and themselves. They may co-operate in this, fully realizing what they are about and the ultimate aim of their actions, because it is a matter that concerns themselves. They may even find themselves in opposition to that aim and thus even become instruments of the State, for it is towards making them a reality that the action of the State tends. And yet they are not (as held by the individualistic utilitarians or the school of Kant) wholes that are self-sufficing and that the State should merely respect, since it is through the State, and the State alone, that they have a moral existence.

[. . .]

MORALS OF CONTRACTUAL RELATIONS

For contracts to be accepted as morally binding, we have come to require not only that they should be by consent, but that they respect the rights of the contracting parties. The very first of these rights is that things and services should not be given except at the fair price. We disapprove any contract with a 'lion's share' in it, that is, one that favours one party unduly at the expense of the other; therefore we hold that the society is not bound to enforce it or, at least, ought not to enforce it as fully as one that is equitable, since it does not call for an

[2]N.B.'without becoming, as it were, a mystic concept of State'.

equal respect. [. . .]

Quite apart from the contract of usury, all regulations that are introduced in industrial law bear witness to the same need. These are designed to prevent the employer from abusing his position to get labour out of the workman on terms too much against his interests, that is to say, on terms that do not equate his true value. This is why we get proposals, whether justified of not, to fix a firm minimum wage. These are evidence that not every contract by consent is in our view one that is valid and just, even when there has been no actual coercion. In default of any regulations for a minimum wage, there are now provisions in the laws of several European countries that require the employer to insure the workman against sickness, old age and accidents. It was whilst this mood prevailed that our recent law was passed on industrial accidents. It is one of the many means employed by the legislative assembly to make the contract of labour less unjust. Wages are not fixed, but the employer is obliged to guarantee certain specific advantages to his employees. Protests are made and it is said this really amounts to giving privileges to the worker. In one sense this is quite true, but these are meant to counterbalance in part those other privileges enjoyed by the employer which leave him free to undervalue at will the services of the worker. I will not debate the usefulness attributed to these practices. It may be they are not the best or they may even work against the aim in view. No matter. It is enough to recognize the moral impulses that inspired them and whose reality they prove.

Everything goes to shew that we are not at the end of this development and that our demands on this score are rapidly growing. The feeling of human sympathy, indeed, which is their determining cause, is bound to gather greater force as it takes on a more egalitarian character. We are still inclined, under the influence of all kinds of prejudices inherited from the past, not to consider men of different classes from the same point of view. We are more sensitive to the distresses and undeserved hardships that a man of a superior class may undergo, who has important duties, than to the distress and burdens of those given up to humbler duties and labours. Everything leads us to suppose that this discrepancy in our way of sympathizing with different classes of people will tend gradually to fade away; that the misfortunes of one class will no longer seem more deplorable than the distresses of the other; that we shall consider them both as equally painful, since both are aspects of human suffering. Therefore we shall now be trying to take stronger measures to ensure that the contractual system shall hold an even balance between the two sides. We shall demand greater justice in contracts. I will not go so far as to say that the day will ever come when this justice will be absolute, when values will be exactly equated as between services exchanged. It might be said, and with reason, that it is not possible to carry it to the extreme limit. Are there not services which are beyond any adequate remuneration? Moreover, only a rough attempt can be made to make things square absolutely. But certainly, the balance of values that exists to-day still does not satisfy our present ideas of justice, and the more we advance the more we shall try to get near to the correct ratio. No one can set any limits to this development.

Now the supreme obstacle it comes up against is the institution of inheritance. It is obvious that inheritance, by creating inequalities amongst men from birth, that are unrelated to merit or services, invalidates the whole contractual system at its very roots. What indeed is the fundamental condition for ensuring the reciprocity of contracted services? It is this: for each to hold his own in this kind of duel from which the contract issues, and in the course of which the terms of exchange are fixed; the weapons of the contracting parties must match as nearly as possible. Then, and then alone, there will be neither victor nor vanquished; this means that things will be exchanged so as to balance exactly and to be equal in value. What the one receives will be equivalent to what he gives and vice versa. Conversely, a privileged contracting party could make use of the advantage he holds to impose his will on the other and oblige him to give the thing or service being exchanged at a price below its true value. If, for instance, the one contracts to obtain something to live on, and the other only to obtain something to live better on, it is clear that the force of resistance of the latter will far exceed that of the former, by the fact that he can drop the idea of contracting if he fails to get the terms he wants. The other cannot do this. He is therefore obliged to yield and to submit to what is laid down for him.

Now inheritance as an institution results in men being born either rich or poor. that is to say, there are two main classes in society, linked by all sorts of intermediate classes: the one which in order to live has to make its services acceptable to the other at whatever the cost; the other class which can do without these services, because it can call on certain resources, which may, however, not be equal to the services rendered by those who have them to offer. Therefore as long as such sharp class differences exist in society, fairly effective palliatives may lessen the injustice of contracts; but in principle, the system operates in conditions which do not allow of justice. It is not only to cover certain particular points that 'lion's share' contracts can be entered into, but the contract represents the 'lion's share' system as far as any relations of the two classes are concerned. It is the general lines on which the services of those not favoured by fortune are assessed that seem unjust, because the conditions stand in the way of their being reckoned at their true social value. The inherited fortune loads the scales and upsets the balance. It is in opposition to this inequitable assessment and to a whole state of society that allows it to happen, that we get the growing revolt of men's conscience. It is true that over the centuries, the injustice could be accepted without revolt because the demand for equality was less. To-day, however, it conflicts only too obviously with the attitide which is found underlying our morality.

[. . .]

We have seen moreover that inheritance *ab intestat,* a survival of the old right of family joint ownership, is to-day an archaic survival and without justification. It no longer corresponds to anything in our ethics and could be abolished without disturbing the moral structure of our societies in any way. As far as testamentary inheritance goes, it seems a more delicate matter. It is not because it is more easily reconciled with the principle we have raised. It offends the spirit of justice as much as inheritance *ab intestat* does and creates the same inequalities. Nowadays, we no longer allow a man to bequeath by will the titles or rank he acquired or the offices held in his lifetime. Why should property be any the more transferable? The position in society we have succeeded in attaining is at least as much our own creation as our fortune. If the law prohibits our disposing of the first, why should it be any different concerning the second — that is, property? Such a limitation to the right of disposal is in no way an attack on the individual concept of property — on the contrary. For individual property is property that begins and ends with the individual. It is the hereditary transference, whether by a man's Will or otherwise, that is contrary to the spirit of individualism. There are no real difficulties on this point, except when it is a question of testamentary inheritance in direct descent. Here a kind of conflict arises between our sense of justice and certain family customs that are very deeply rooted. It is clear that at the present day the idea that we could be prevented from leaving our possessions to our children would meet with very lively resistance. For our work is done quite as much to ensure their happiness as our own. That does not mean that this state of mind does not derive very closely from the present structure of property. Let us grant that there is a transfer by inheritance and in consequence an initial inequality in the economic status of individuals at the time they enter the life of the society. We then attempt to make this inequality have as little disadvantage as possible for the human beings with whom we have the closest ties; we go further, and try to make it even a positive advantage. Hence our anxiety to work for them. But if equality were the rule, this need would be of far less concern to us. For the peril to them of facing life with no resources but their own would have disappeared. This peril comes solely from certain people being at present endowed with initial advantages, a fact that places those not so endowed in a position obviously inferior. All the same, it is not un- likely that something would always remain of the right to dispose of property by will. The old institutions never disappear entirely; they only pass into the background and fade away by degrees. This one has played too great a role in history for it to be conceivable that nothing of it should survive. It would only survive, however, in a weakened form. We might for instance imagine that every head of family would have the right to leave to his children specified portions of the heritage. The inequalities that would then continue would be so slight as not to seriously affect the working of the contractual right.

And so, it is beyond us to make any very accurate forecast on this subject, for one factor needed in making it is at present lacking. To whom, indeed, would the wealth go to that each generation would leave without an owner as it left the scene? When there were no longer any heirs either by birth or by right, who would then inherit? The State? It is clearly impossible to concentrate such vast resources in hands that are already so blundering and wasteful. Alternatively, a periodic sharing-out of these things amongst individuals would have to be made, or at the very least of certain things, such as those essential to labour, of the land, for instance. Surely we can imagine some form of auction, when things of this kind would be knocked down to the highest bidder. But it is obvious that the State is too far removed from things and individuals to be able to carry out tasks so vast and so complex with any competence. There would have to be secondary groups, more limited in range and closer to the facts in detail, to be able to fulfil this function. We could hardly choose any better suited to the task than the professional groups. They are well equipped to manage any particular set of interests and could branch out into all parts of the country; at the same time they would take into account the regional differences and purely local affairs. They would satisfy all the conditions for becoming in a sense, in the economic sphere, the heirs of the family.

Reading 10

SOCIALISM

[...]

Science is a study bearing on a delimited portion of reality which it aims at knowing and, if possible understanding. To describe and explain what is and what has been − this is its only job. Speculation about the future is not its affair, although it may seek as its final objective to render this possible.

Socialism, on the contrary, is entirely oriented towards the future. It is above all a plan for the reconstruction of societies, a program for a collective life which does not exist as yet or in the way it is dreamed of, and which is proposed to men as worthy of their preference. It is an ideal. It concerns itself much less with what is or was than what ought to be. Undoubtedly, even under it most utopian forms it never disdained the support of facts, and has even, in more recent times, increasingly affected a certain scientific turn of phrase. It is indisputable that it has thus rendered social science more services perhaps than it

Edited and reprinted with permission from: *Socialism and Saint-Simon,* edited by A. W. Gouldner, translated by C. Sattler, Yellow Springs, Ohio, Antioch Press, and London, Routledge & Kegan Paul, 1959; paperback edn. by Collier-Macmillan, 1962, pp. 39−43, 56−59. Originally published as *Le Socialisme,* Paris, Presses Universitaires de France, 1928.

received from it. For it has aroused reflection, it has stimulated scientific activity, it has instigated research, posed problems, so that in more than one way its history blends with the very history of sociology. Yet, how can one fail to note the enormous disparity between the rare and meager data it borrows from science and the extent of the practical conclusions that it draws, and which are, nevertheless, the heart of the system? It aspires to a complete remolding of the social order. But in order to know what the family, property, political, moral, juridical, and economic organization of the European peoples can and ought to be, even in the near future, it is indispensable to have studied this multitude of instutions and practices in the past, to have searched for the ways in which they varied in history, and for the principal conditions which have determined these variations. And only then will it be possible to ask oneself rationally what they ought to be now – under the present conditions of our collective existence. But all this research is still in its infancy. Several are hardly going enterprises; the most advanced have not yet passed beyond a very rudimentay phase. Since each of these problems is a world in itself, the solution cannot be found in an instant, merely because the need is felt. The bases for a rigorous prediction about the future, especially one of such breadth, are not established. It is necessary that the theoretician himself construct them. Socialism has not taken the time; perhaps one could even say, it did not have the time.

That is why, to speak precisely, there cannot be a scientific socialism. Because, were such a socialism even possible, sciences would be necessary that are not yet developed and which cannot be improvised. The only attitude that science permits in the face of these problems is reservation and circumspection, and socialism can hardly maintain this without lying to itself. And, in fact, socialism has not maintained this attitude. Note even the strongest work – the most systematic, the richest in ideas – that this school has produced: Marx's *Capital*. What statistical data, what historical comparisons, what studies would be indispensable to solve any one of the innumerable questions that are dealt with there! Need we be reminded that an entire theory of value is established in a few lines? The truth is that the facts and observations assembled by theoreticians anxious to document their affirmations are hardly there except to give form to the arguments. The research studies they made were undertaken to establish a doctrine that they had previously conceived, rather than the doctrine being a result of the -research. Almost all had developed before asking science for the help it could lend them. It is fervor that has been the inspiration of all these systems; what gave them life and strength is a thirst for a more perfect justice, pity for the misery of the working classes, a vague sympathy for the travail of contemporary societies, etc. Socialism is not a science, a sociology in miniature – it is a cry of grief, sometimes of anger, uttered by men who feel most keenly our collective *malaise*. Socialism is to the facts which produce is what the groans of a sick man are to the illness with which he is afflicted, to the needs that torment him. But what would one say of a doctor who accepted the replies or desires of his patient as scientific truths? Moreover, the theories ordinarily offered in opposition to socialism are no different in nature and they no more merit the title we refuse the latter. When economists call for *laissez faire*, demanding that the influence of the state be reduced to nothing, that competition be freed of every restraint, they are not basing their claims on laws scientifically developed. The social sciences are still much too young to be able to serve as bases for practical doctrines, which are so vast and of such breadth. Such policies are maintained by needs of another kind – a jealousy of individual autonomy, a love of order, a fear of novelty, misoneism as it is called today. Individualism, like socialism, is above all a ferment which affirms itself, although it may eventually ask Reason for reasons with which to justify itself.

If this is so, then to study socialism as a system of abstract propositions, as a body of scientific theories and to discuss it formally, is to see and show a side of it which is of minor interest. Those aware of what social science must be, of the slow pace of its processes, of the laborious investigations it implies to resolve even the narrowest questions, cannot be fond of these premature solutions, these vast systems so summarily sketched out. One is too aware of the discrepancy that exists between its simple methods and its elaborate conclusions, and one is consequently prompted to scorn the latter. But socialism can be examined in an entirely different light. It is not a scientific formulation of social facts, it is itself a social fact of the highest importance. If it is not a product of science, it is an object of science. As such, we do not have to borrow from socialism such and such a proposition ready made; but we do have to know socialism, and to understand what it is, where it comes from, and where it is going.

It is interesting to study socialism from this point of view, for two reasons. First, one can hope that it will aid us in understanding the social conditions which gave rise to it. For precisely because it derives from certain conditions, socialism manifests and expresses them in its own way, and thereby gives us another means of viewing them. It is certainly not that socialism reflects these conditions accurately. On the contrary, for the reasons mentioned above, we can be certain that it refracts them involuntarily and give us only an unfaithful impression, just as a sick man faultily interprets the feelings that he experiences and most often attributes them to a cause which is not the true one. But these feelings, such as they are, have their interest, and the clinician notes them with great care and takes them seriously. They are an element in the diagnosis, and an important one. For example, he is not indifferent as to where they are felt, when they began. In the same way, it is highly material to determine the epoch when socialism began to appear. It is a cry of collective anguish, let us say. Well then, it is essential to fix the moment when this cry was uttered for the first time. For if we see it as a present fact related to entirely new social conditions, or, on the contrary, as a simple recurrence – at the most a variant of the lamentations that the wretched of all epochs and societies have made heard (eternal clains of the poor against the rich), we will judge its tendencies quite differently. In the second case, we will be led to believe that these grievances can no more be terminated than human misery can end. They will be thought of as a kind of chronic illness of humanity which, from time to time in the course of history and under the influence of transitory circumstances, seems to become more acute and grievous, but which always ends by at last abating; then one will strive only to discover some anodyne to lull it into security again. If, on the contrary, we find that it is of recent date, that it is related to a situation without analogy in history, we can no longer assume it is a chronic condition and are less ready to take such a view.

But it is not only to diagnose the nature of the illness that this study of socialism promises to be instructive; it is, also, in order to find appropriate remedies. To be sure, we can be certain in advance that the remedies are not precisely those sought by the systems, just as the drink demanded by a feverish patient is not necessarily what he needs. Still, the needs that he does feel do not cease to serve as some guide in the treatment. They are never without some cause, and sometimes it is best to satisfy them. For the same reason, it is important to know what social rearrangements, that is, what remedies, the suffering masses of society have spontaneously and instinctively conceived of, however unscientific their elaboration might have been. This is what socialist theories express. [. . .]

After having discussed the definitions at hand and noted their inadequacy, we ourselves searched for the signs by which one could recognize socialism and distinguish it from what it was not, and by an objective comparison of the different doctrines concerned with social problems, we came to the following formula: one calls socialist those theories which demand a more or less complete connection of all economic functions or of certain of them, though diffused, with the directing and knowing organs of society.

This definition calls for a few comments.

We have already observed that we were saying "connection" and not "subordination," and one cannot too strongly stress this difference, which is essential. Socialists do not demand that the economic life be put into the hands of the state, but into contact with it. On the contrary, they declare that it should react on the state at least as much as — if not more than — the latter acts on it. In their thinking, this rapport should have the effect, not of subordinating industrial and commercial interests to "political" interests, but rather of elevating the former to the rank of the latter. For, once this constant communication is assured, these economic interests would affect the functioning of the government organ much more profoundly than today and contribute in much larger measure to determining its course. Very far from relegating economic interests to second place, it would much rather be a question of calling upon them to play, in the whole of social life, a considerably more important role than is permitted today, when precisely because of their distance from the directing centers of society, they can activate the latter only feebly and intermittently. Even according to the most celebrated theoreticians of socialism, the state as we know it would disappear and no longer be the central point of economic life — rather than economic life being absorbed by the state. For this reason, in the definition, we have not used the term "state," but the expression — expanded and somewhat figurative — "the knowing and managing organs of society." In the doctrine of Marx, for example, the state such as it is — that is to say, insofar as it has a specific role, and represents interests which are superior, *sui generis*, to those of commerce and industry, historic traditions, common beliefs and a religious or other nature, etc. — would no longer exist. Purely political functions, which today are its special sphere, would no longer have a *raison d'être*, and there would be only economic functions. It would no longer be called by the same name, which is why we have had to resort to a more general term. [. . .]

Comparing this definition of the concept with those generally held of socialism, we can now ascertain the differences. Thus, according to the terms of our formula the theories which recommend, as a remedy for the evils suffered by present societies, a greater development of charitable and provident institutions (not only private, but public), would not be called socialist, although very often one does call them this — either to attack or to defend them. But it is not that our definition is in error; it is that by so calling them one gives them an unfitting name. For, however generous they may be, however useful it may be to put them into practice − which is not under discussion − they do not correspond at all to the needs and thoughts socialism has awakened and expresses. By characterizing them as socialist one mingles, within a single category and identical name, very different things. To establish welfare projects alongside of economic life, is not to bind the latter to public life. The diffuse state in which industrial and commercial functions are found does not diminish because one creates welfare funds to ameliorate the fortunes of those who, temporarily or forever, have ceased to fulfill these functions. Socialism is essentially a movement to organize, but charity organizes nothing. It maintains the *status quo;* it can only attenuate the individual suffering that this lack of organization engenders. By this new example, we can see how important it is to ascertain carefully the meaning of the word if one does not wish to be mistaken about the nature of the thing, or the significance of the practical measures taken or recommended.

Another important remark our definition gives rise to is that neither class war, nor concern about rendering economic relations more equitable and even more favorable for workers, figures in it. Far from being the whole of socialism, these characteristics do not even represent an essential element of it, nor are they *sui generis*, part of it. We are, it is true, so accustomed to an entirely different conception that at first such a statement is rather surprising and could arouse doubts as to the exactness of our definition. Do not both partisans and adversaries constantly present socialism to us as the philosophy of the working classes? But it is now easy to see that this tendency is far from the only one which inspires it but is actually only a particular, and is a derived form of the more general tendency (in the service of which we have expressed it). In reality, amelioration of the workers' fate is only one goal that socialism desires from the economic organization it demands, just as class war is only one of the means by which this reorganization could result, one aspect of the historic development producing it.

And in fact, what is it, according to socialists that causes the inferiority of the working classes and the injustice whose victims it declares them to be? It is that they are placed in direct dependence, not on society in general, but on a particular class powerful enough to impose its own wishes on them. That is, the "capitalists." The workers do not do business directly with society; it is not the latter which directly remunerates them − it is the capitalist. But the last is a mere individual who as such concerns himself − and that legitimately − not with social interest but with its own. Thus, the services he buys he seeks to pay for not according to what they are worth socially — that is to say, according to the exact degree of usefulness they have for society — but at the least possible price. But in his hands he has a weapon that permits him to force those who live only by their labor to sell him the product for less than it is really worth. This is his capital. He can live, if not indefinitely, at least for a long while, on his accumulated wealth, which he consumes instead of using to give work to the laborers. He purchases their help only if he wishes and when he wishes, whereas they, on the contrary, cannot wait. They must sell without delay the only thing they have to sell, since, by definition, they have no other means of subsistence. So they are obliged to yield in some degree to the demands of him who pays them, to reduce their own demands below what they should be if public interest alone served as the measure of value, and consequently are forced to allow themselves to be hurt. I do not have to evaluate here whether this preponderance of capital is real or if, as orthodox economists say, the competition capitalists create among themselves eliminates it. It is enough to present the socialist argument without judging it.

These premises posed, it is clear that the only means of at least tempering this subjection and ameliorating this state of affairs, is to moderate the power of capital by another [force] which at first may be of equal or superior strength but which [in addition] can make its action felt in conformity with the general interests of society. For it would be altogether useless to have another individual and private force intervene in the economic mechanism. This would be to replace with another kind — and not to suppress — the slavery from which the proletariat suffers. Therefore, only the state is capable of playing the role of moderator. But for that it is essential that the economic media cease to operate outside of it, without the state being aware of them. On the contrary, by means of a continuing communication the state must know what is happening, and in turn to make its own action known. If one wishes to go still further, if one intends not only to attenuate but put a radical stop to this situation, it is necessary to completely suppress the medium of the capitalist who, by wedging himself between worker and society, prevents labor from being properly appreciated and rewarded according to its social value. This last must be directly evaluated and recompensed — if not by the community (which is practically impossible), then at least by the social agency which normally represents it. This is to say that the capitalist class under these conditions must disappear, that the state fulfill these functions at the same time as it is placed in direct relation with the working class, and in consequence, must become the center of economic life. The improvement of the workers' lot is thus not a special objective; it is but one of the consequences that the attachment of economic activities to the managing agents of society must produce. And in socialist thought, this improvement will be all the more complete as the connection itself is stronger. In this there are not two paths; one, which would aim at the organization of economic life, and the other, which would strive to make the situation of the great majority less noxious. The second is but an outcome of the first. In other words, according to socialism there is presently an entire segment of the economic world which is not truly and directly integrated into society. This is the working class, not the capitalists. They are not full-fledged members of society, since they participate in the community's life only through an imposed medium which, having its own nature, prevents them from acting upon society and receiving benefits from it in a measure and manner consistent with the social value of their services. It is this which creates the situation they are said to suffer from. What they desire, consequently, when they demand better treatment, is to be no longer kept at a distance from the centers presiding over collective life but be bound to them more or less intimately. The material changes they hope for are only one form and result of this more complete integration.

Thus our definition actually takes into account these special concerns which at first did not seem to enter; only they are now in their proper place — which is a secondary one. Socialism does not reduce itself to a question of wages, or — as they say — the stomach. It is above all an aspiration for a rearrangement of the social structure, by relocating the industrial set-up in the totality of the social organism, drawing it out of the shadow where it was functioning automatically, summoning it to the light and to the control of the conscience.

Part Seven

Education

Reading 11

THE EVOLUTION OF
EDUCATIONAL THOUGHT

[. . .]

Science is the great novelty of our century, and for all those who experience it as such, scientific culture seems to form the basis of all culture whatsoever. Should we notice that we are short of practical people with technical skills, then we shall conclude that the aim of education is to develop practical capabilities. It is this sort of situation which gives rise to educational theories which are exaggerated, one-sided and incomplete, expressing only temporary needs and transitory aspirations, theories which in any case cannot long endure, for they soon generate others to correct, complete and modify them. The man of his times is a man who is dominated by the needs and inclinations of the moment, and these are always one-sided and tomorrow will be replaced by others. The result is all sorts of clashes and revolutions which can do nothing but harm to the steady process of evolution. What we need to understand is not the man of the moment, man as we experience him at a particular point in time, influenced as we are by

Edited and reprinted with permission from: *The Evolution of Educational Thought*, translated by P. Collins, London, Routledge & Kegan Paul, 1977, pp. 12–13, 205–207, 326–330. From the French *L'Evolution pédagogique en France*, Paris, Presses Universitaires de France, 1938.

momentary needs and passions, but rather man in his totality throughout time.

To do this we need to cease studying man at a particular moment and instead try to consider him against the background of the whole process of his development. Instead of confining ourselves to our own particular age, we must on the contrary escape from it in order to escape from ourselves, from our narrow-minded points of view, which are both partial and partisan. And that is precisely why a study of the history of education is so important and worthwhile. Instead of starting out by what the contemporary ideal ought to be we must transport ourselves to the other end of the historical time-scale; we must strive to understand the educational ideology most remote in time from our own, the one which was the first to be elaborated in European culture. We will study it, describe it and, as far as we are able, explain it. Then, step by step, we will follow the series of changes which it has undergone, parallel to changes in society itself, until finally we arrive at the contemporary situation. That is where we must end, not where we must begin; and when, by travelling along this road, we arrive at the present-day situation it will appear in a light quite different from that in which we would have seen it, had we abandoned ourselves at once and unreservedly to our contemporary passions and prejudices. In this way we shall avoid the risk of succumbing to the prestigious influence exercised by transitory passions and the predilections, because these will be counter-balanced by the newly acquired sensitivity to differences in needs and necessities – all equally legitmate – with which the study of history will have furnished us. Thus the problem, instead of being arbitrarily over-simplified, wil become susceptible of a dispassionate examination, in all its complexity and in a form which is no less relevant for the student of the social ethos of our own age than it is for the historian.

This kind of historical enquiry will even on occasions enable us to revise our ideas about history itself. For the development of educational theory, like all human development, has been far from following a steady, regular course. In the course of the struggles and conflicts which have arisen between opposing sets of ideas, it has often happened that basically sound ideas have floundered, whereas, judged from the point of view of their intrinsic worth, they ought to have survived. Here as elsewhere the struggle for survival has led to results which are only crude and approximate. In general it is the best adapted and the most gifted which survive, but as against that, this whole history is littered with a multitude of lamentable and unjustified triumphs, deaths and defeats. How many healthy ideas which ought to have survived to maturity have been cut down in their prime! New educational theories — no less than moral or political ones — are so full of the fire and energy of youth that they adopt a stance of violent aggressiveness towards those which they seek to replace. They regard them as implacable enemies, so conscious are they of the burning hostility which divides them, and they strive to the limits of their capacity to subdue and, as far as possible, exterminate them. The champions of new ideas will willingly believe that there is nothing worth preserving in the older ideas which are really their progenitors and allies, since it is from them that they descend. The present does battle with the past, despite the fact that it derives from it and constitutes its continuation. Thus it is that aspects of the past disappear which could have and should have become standard features of the present and the future.

[. . .]

Thus the educational ideas of the Humanists were not the result of simple accidents; they derived rather from a fact whose influence on the moral history of our country it is difficult to exaggerate; I refer to the establishment of polite society. If France did indeed become from the sixteenth century onwards a centre of literary life and intellectual activity this was because, at this same period, there had developed amongst us a select society, a society of intellectually cultivated people to whom our writers addressed themselves. It was the ideas and the tastes of this society which they communicated, and it was for this society that they wrote and for it that they thought. It was here in this particular environment that the driving force of our civilization from the sixteenth century to the middle of the eighteenth century was generated. The object of education as Erasmus conceived of it was to prepare men for this special and restricted society.

Here too we can see the essential character and at the same time the radical flaw of this educational theory. It is essentially aristocratic in nature. The kind of society which it seeks to fashion is always centred around a court, and its members are always drawn from the ranks of the aristocracy or at least from the leisured classes. And it was indeed here and here alone that the fine flowering of elegance and culture could take place, the nurturing and development of which was regarded as more important than anything else. Neither Erasmus nor Vives had any awareness that beyond this small world, which for all its brilliance was very limited, there were vast masses who should not have been neglected, and for whom education should have raised their intellectual and moral standards and improved their material condition.

When such a thought does occur to them it disappears again very quickly without their thinking it is necessary to examine it at length. Since he realises that this expensive education is not suitable for everyone Erasmus wonders what the poor will do; the answer which he gives to this objection is utterly simple: 'You ask,' he says, 'what the poor will be able to do. How will those who can scarcely feed their children be able to give them over a sustained period of time the right kind of education? To this I can only reply by quoting the words of the comic writer: "You can't ask that what we are capable of achieving should be as great as what we would like to achieve". We are expounding the best way of bringing up a child, we cannot produce the means of realising this ideal.' He restricts himself to expressing the wish that the rich will come to the help of those who are well-endowed intellectually but who would be prevented by poverty from developing their aptitudes. He does not even seem to realise that even if this education was made available to everybody the difficulty would not be resolved; for this generalised education would not meet the needs of the majority. For the majority the supreme need is survival; and what is needed in order to survive is not the art of subtle speech, it is the art of sound thinking so that one knows how to act. In order to struggle effectively in the world of persons and the world of things, more substantial weapons are needed than those glittering decorations with which the Humanist educationalists were concerned to adorn the mind to the exclusion of anything else.

Think how much more Scholasticism, for all its abstractness, was imbued with a more practical, more realistic and more social spirit. The fact is that dialectic answered real needs. Intellectual conflict and competition between ideas constitutes a genuinely important part of life. The strength and virility which was acquired by thought as a result of such arduous gymnastics were capable of being used in the service of socially useful ends. Thus we must be aware of thinking that the mediaeval schools served dnly to produce dreamers, seekers after quintesscences, the useless pettifogging quibblers. The truth is quite the opposite. It was there that the statesmen, the ecclesiastical dignitaries, and the administrators of the day were brought up. This training which has been so denigrated created men of action. It was the education recommended by Erasmus which forms a totally inadequate preparation for life. Rhetoric supplants dialectic. Now, if rhetoric had good reason for featuring in the education of the classical world, where the practice of eloquence constituted not only a career but the most important career, this was by no means the case in the sixteenth century when it played only a very small part in the serious business of life. A theory of education which made rhetoric the principal academic discipline could thus only develop qualities related to the luxuries of existence and not at all to its necessities.

[...]

If there is one principle which to us appears essential to all forms of thought, it is the principle of non-contradiction. If a judgment is self-contradictory we regard it as being a denial of itself and consequently worthless. Now, there are in existence symbolic systems which in the course of history have played a role as great as, if not greater than, that of science but in which this principle is violated at every turn: I refer to the symbolic systems of religion. Myths constantly treat of beings which at the same moment are both themselves and not themselves, which are at once single and double, spiritual and material. The notion of a single substance capable of infinite division while yet neither diminishing nor ceasing to be the same unified whole in each of its parts; this notion, although it violates the principle of the conservation of matter and energy, is at the root of a wide variety of beliefs and practices which even today can be found amongst a large number of different peoples. There are even different systems of logic which have followed one another or co-existed but which were by no means arbitrary, being all of them equally grounded in the nature of reality, that is in the nature of different societies. For, in proportion as different societies needed to give expression to the consciousness of themselves and the world in religious and mythical forms, in proportion as some religious system was indispensable to their survival, there emerged a parallel need to operate a system of logic which necessarily could not be that which informs scientific thought.

If this is the case then it is easy to see that Humanism was totally misguided in its attempt to teach children about human nature in general, for there is simply no such thing. Human nature is not a specific reality which one finds more in evidence here rather than there, in this literature or that civilisation, and which consequently has a tangibility of its own. It is rather a construct of the human mind and an arbitrary construct at that; for we have absolutely no means of saying what it consists of, how it is constituted, or where it begins and ends. We have just seen in fact that feelings which we regard as the most supremely natural, and ideas which we would be inclined to regard as indispensable to the normal functioning of any kind of thought, have, as a matter of quite normal course, been completely absent smongst whole peoples.

In fact 'man', as Humanist teachers portrayed and continue to portray him, was no more than the product of a synthesis between Christian, Roman and Greek ideals; and it was these three ideals which were used to mould him, because it was these three ideals which had moulded the consciousness of those who expounded him. This explains why there is something abstract and relatively universal about him, for he is the product of a kind of spontaneous generalisation. Yet for all its generality, this ideal is still idiosyncratic and transitory, expressing the very special circumstances in which European civilisation developed, and especially that of our own people. There is consequently no justification whatsoever for presenting it as the only ideal conception of man, the only one which expresses the true nature of man; it stands, on the contrary, in very definite causal relationship to a particular time and a particular place. If then we wish to give our pupils some genuinely objective notion of what man is really like, and not merely a portrait of how he was ideally conceived at some particular moment of history, we shall have to set about it quite differently. We shall have to find some means of making him aware not only of what is constant in human nature but also of that element in it which is irreducibly diverse.

If human nature is so diverse, if it is liable to variations and transformations the possible multiplicity of which cannot be determined *a priori*, then unquestionably we can no longer continue to conceive of it as a single reality specifiable in clear-cut categories, capable of being formulated once and for all time. The reason this view of the matter is so attractive to us is the tendency, very deep-rooted within us, to think that the only true form of humanity, genuinely worthy of the name, is that which emerges in those civilisations which we have got into the habit of investing with the significance of a private cult. But the truth is that if, in our attempt to form a picture of man as he really is, we concentrate solely on one particular and allegedly superior people, our view of man becomes severely narrow and distorted. Of course, there is a sense in which we can describe this form of humanity as superior to that of less advanced peoples, but this does not make these latter any less human. All the feelings, all the states of mind which find expression even in inferior cultures, are nevertheless still essentially human, deriving from human nature, and manifesting certain aspects of it: they show us what it is capable of becoming and creating under specific circumstances. In the myths, legends and skills of even the most primitive peoples there are involved highly complex mental processes, which sometimes shed more light on the mechanisms of the human mind than the more self-conscious intellectual operations on which the positive sciences are based.

A soon as we have fully grasped the infinite variety of the systems of thought which man has thus developed from the raw material of basic human nature, we realise that it is impossible to say, at any particular point in history: here is manifested the essence of human nature; here we can see how it is constituted. For the immense wealth of what has been produced in the past is precisely what makes it illegitimate for us to assign a limit in advance to what man is capable of producing in the future; or to assume that a time will come when, man's capacity for creative innovation being exhausted, he will be doomed merely to repeat himself throughout all eternity. Thus we come to conceive of man not as an agglomeration of finite specifiable elements, but rather as an infinitely flexible, protean force, capable of appearing in innumerable guises, according to the perennially changing demands of his circumstances. Far from its being the case that humanity in its entirety achieves full fruition at some one particular moment of history, there is in each of us a multitude of unrealised potentialities, seeds which may be dormant in the ground for ever, but which may also blossom into life if called upon by the force of circumstance. The *personae* which humanity currently adopts may once again be submerged; new ones may be born and old ones, fallen into desuetude, may be reborn in new forms adapted to the new conditions of life. This is the picture of man which history paints for us; and it differs dramatically from that implied in and propagated by the traditional Humanist education.

But the value of seeing man this way is not of a purely theoretical kind; for, as we should expect, our conception of man is also capable of affecting our conduct.

One reason why we often shy away from relatively novel social enterprises, even when we are more or less lucidly aware that they are essential (and this incidentally is why even the most acute minds are inclined to be neophobic), is that we conceive of human nature as something which is narrowly and rigidly circumscribed; and consequently it appears to us to be essentially hostile to any innovation of real significance. The limits within which it is capable of change seem to us to be extremely narrow. We believe, for example, that the conception of human desire on which we base our present-day system of ethics describes essential and immutable features of human nature; and consequently any reform which depends on a relatively radical modification of human desires most easily strikes us as a dangerous and impracticable utopianism. While it is obvious that human nature cannot become just anything at all, it is equally certain that the limits to what it can become are set very much farther back than is suggested by the crude examination on which popular opinion is based. It is only because we have got so used to it that the moral order under which we live appears to us to be the only one possible; history demonstrates that it is essentially transistory in character. For by showing that this moral order came into being at a particular time under particular circumstances, history justifies us in believing that the day may eventually come when it will give way to a different moral order based on different ethical principles. Amongst all the advances accomplished in the past, there is scarcely one to which this *ne plus ultra* argument has not been raised in opposition; and yet historically evolution has always played havoc with the restrictions which men have sought to impose on it. When we reflect on these past experiences, we ought to become very suspicious of claims to be able to restrict the possible scope of evolution in the future.

To sum up, human nature as it manifests itself in history is above all something which we can and should credit with amazing flexibility and fecundity. We need not fear that this conviction will cause men's minds to swing abruptly from neophobia, which is one kind of evil, to what is a different but no lesser evil, namely revolutionary excess. What history teaches us is that man does not charge arbitrarily; he does not transform himself at will on hearing the voices of inspired prophets. The reason is that all change, in colliding with the inherited institutions of the past, is inevitably hard and laborious; consequently it only takes place in response to the demands of necessity. For change to be brought about it is not enough that it should be seen as desirable; it must be the product of changes within the whole network of diverse causal relationships which determine the situation of man.

Another practical consequence of this view consists in impressing upon us the fact (which follows from the previous point) of how little we know ourselves. When we contemplate the history of the modes of human behaviour, thought and feeling, all of which are so different from one another and from those to which we are accustomed, and yet which are characteristically human, rooted in human nature and expressive of it, how can we fail to realise that we contain within us hidden depths where unknown powers slumber but which from time to time may be aroused according to the demands of circumstances? This extended and expanded view of humanity makes us realise more clearly how impoverished, flimsy and deceptive is the one yielded by direct observation of ourselves; for we must candidly admit that there exists in us something of all these styles of humanity which have historically succeeded one another, even if we are not currently sensible of the fact. These men of former ages were men like ourselves, and it is consequently impossible that their nature should be completely foreign to us. Similarly, there live in us, as it were, other men than those with whom we are familiar. This proposition is confirmed by the findings of modern psychology, which reveal the existence of an unconscious psychic life beyond that of consciousness; a life which science alone is gradually managing to uncover, thanks to its special methods of investigation.

But the important thing to see is how much more convincing is the historical evidence for this proposition. For history exposes us to a large part of all these unknown riches which we bear with us. It enables us to become concretely aware of them. We will act quite differently depending on whether we believe that we can attain complete self-knowledge by a simple act of self-examination, or whether we realise, rather, that our most apparent characteristics are also the most superficial. For in the latter case we are less liable to yield to motives, ideas and feelings which brush against our consciousness as if they were the whole of ourselves, whereas we know that we are in fact made up of much else besides, which we do not directly perceive but which it is nonetheless important to take into account. We become aware that to achieve real self-knowledge, and in consequence to act knowing what we are about, we must approach the matter in a quite different way: we must treat ourselves as an unknown quantity, whose nature and character we must seek to grasp by examining (as is the case with external things) the objective phenomena which express it, and not by giving heed to those so transitory and unreliable impressions of inner feelings.

Reading 12

MORAL EDUCATION

The practical reason for the limitations imposed by discipline are not so immediately apparent. It seems to imply a violence against human nature, to limit man, to place obstacles in the path of his free development, is this not to prevent him from fulfilling himself? But we have seen that this limitation is a condition of our happiness and moral health. Man, in fact, is made for life in a determinate, limited environment, however extended it may be; the sum total of his life activities is aimed at adapting to this milieu or adapting it to his needs. Thus, the behaviour required of us shares in this same determination. To live is to put ourselves in harmony with the physical world surrounding us and with the social world of which we are members; however extended their realms, they are nevertheless limited. The goals we normally seek are equally delimited, and we are not free to transcend the limits without placing ourselves at odds with nature. At each moment of time, our hopes, our feelings of all sorts must be within bounds. The function of discipline is to guarantee such restraint. If such necessary limits are lacking, if the moral forces surrounding us can no longer contain or

Edited and reprinted with permission from: *Moral Education,* translated by E. K. Wilson and H. Schnurer, New York, Free Press, 1961. Originally *L'Education morale,* Paris, Alcan, 1925, pp. 48–53.

moderate our passions, human conduct − being no longer constrained − loses itself in the void, the emptiness of which is disguised and adorned with the specious label of the infinite.

Discipline is thus useful, not only in the interests of society and as the indispensable means without which regular cooperation would be impossible, but for the welfare of the individual himself. By means of discipline we learn the control of desire without which man could not achieve happiness. Hence, it even contributes in large measure to the development of that which is of fundamental importance for each of us: our personality. The capacity for containing our inclinations, for restraining ourselves − the ability that we acquire in the school of moral discipline − is the indispensable condition for the emergence of reflective, individual will. The rule, because it teaches us to restrain and master ourselves, is a means of emancipation and of freedom. Above all, in democratic societies like ours is it essential to teach the child this wholesome self-control. For, since in some measure the conventional restraints are no longer effective − barriers which in societies differently organized rigorously restrict people's desires and ambitions − there remains only moral discipline to provide the necessary regulatory influence. Because, in principle, all vocations are available to everybody, the drive to get ahead is more readily stimulated and inflamed beyond all measure to the point of knowing almost no limits.

Education must help the child understand at an early point that, beyond certain contrived boundaries that constitute the historical framework of justice, there are limits based on the nature of things, that is to say, in the nature of each of us. This has nothing to do with insidiously inculcating a spirit of resignation in the child; or curbing his legitimate ambitions; or preventing him from seeing the conditions existing around him. Such proposals would contradict the very principles of our social system. But he must be made to understand that the way to be happy is to set proximate and realizable goals, corresponding to the nature of each person and not to attempt to reach objectives by straining neurotically and unhappily toward infinitely distant and consequently inaccesible goals. Without trying to hide the injustices of the world − injustices that always exist − we must make the child appreciate that he cannot rely for happiness upon unlimited power, knowledge, or wealth; but that it can be found in very diverse situations, that each of us has his sorrows as well as his joys, that the important thing is to discover a goal compatible with one's abilities, one which allows him to realize his nature without seeking to surpass it in the same manner, thrusting it violently and artificially beyond its natural limits. There is a whole cluster of mental attitudes that the school should help the child acquire, not because they are in the interests of this or that regime, but because they are sound and will have the most fortunate influence on the general welfare. Let us suggest, further, that moral forces guard against forces of brutality and ignorance. Finally, we must not see in the preference for control certain indescribable tendencies toward stagnation. To move toward clear-cut objectives, one after another, is to move ahead in uninterrupted fashion and not to be immobilized. It is not a matter of knowing whether one must move or not, but at what speed and in what fashion.

Thus, we come to the point of justifying discipline rationally, in terms of its utility, as well as the more obvious aspects of morality. However, we must note that our conception of its function is altogether different from that of certain recognized apologists. In fact, it often happens that, to demonstrate the beneficent results of morality, such apologists rely on a principle that I have criticized: they invoke the support of those who see in discipline only a regrettable, if necessary, evil. Like Bentham and the utilitarians, they take it as self-evident that discipline does violence to human nature; but, rather than concluding that such opposition to man's nature is evil, they consider that it is good because they judge man's nature to be evil. From this point of view, nature is the cause, the flesh is the source of sin and evil. It is not given to a man, then, to develop his nature but, on the contrary, he must triumph over it, he must vanquish it, silence its demands. It only provides him the occasion for a beautiful struggle, an heroic effort against himself. Discipline is precisely the means of this victory. Such is the ascetic conception of discipline as it is preached by certain religions.

The idea I have proposed to you is quite otherwise. If we believe that discipline is useful, indeed necessary for the individual, it is because it seems to us demanded by nature itself. It is the way in which nature realizes itself normally, not a way of minimizing or destroying nature. Like everything else, man is a limited being: he is part of a whole. Physically, he is part of the universe; morally, he is part of society. Hence, he cannot, without violating his nature, try to supersede the limits imposed on every hand. Indeed, everything that is most basic in him partakes of this quality of partialness or particularity. To say that one is a person is to say that he is distinct from all others; this distinction implies limitation. If, then, from our point of view, discipline is good, it is not that we regard the work of nature with a rebellious eye, or that we see here a diabolical scheme that must be foiled; but that man's nature cannot be itself except as it is disciplined. If we deem it essential that natural inclinations be held within certain bounds, it is not because that nature seems to us bad, or because we would deny the right to gratification; on the contrary, it is because otherwise such natural inclinations could have no hope of the satisfaction they merit. Thus, there follows this first practical consequence: asceticism is not good in and of itself.

From this first difference between the two conceptions, others may be derived that are no less significant. If discipline is a means through which man realizes his nature, it must change as that nature changes through time. To the extent of historical progress and as a result of civilization, human nature becomes stronger and more vigorous with greater need of expression; this is why it is normal for the range of human activity to expand for the boundaries of our intellectual, moral, and emotional horizons always to roll farther away. Hence, the arrogance of systems of thought — whether artistic, scientific, or in the realm of human welfare — which would prohibit us from going beyond the points reached by our fathers, or would wish us to return there. The normal boundary line is in a state of continual becoming, and any doctrine which, under the authority of absolute principles, would undertake to fix it immutably, once and for all, must sooner or later run up against the force of the changing nature of things.

Not only does the content of discipline change, but also the way it is and should be inculcated. Not only does man's range of behavior change, but the forces that set limits are not absolutely the same at different historical periods. In the lower societies, since social organization is very simple, morality takes on the same character, consequently, it is neither necessary nor even possible that the nature of discipline be clearly elucidated. This same simplicity of moral behavior makes it easy to transform such behavior into habits, mechanically carried out; under these conditions, such automatism poses no difficulties. Since social life is quite self-consistent, differing but little from one place to another, or from one moment in time to another, custom and unreflective tradition are quite adequate. Indeed, custom and tradition have such power and prestige as to leave no place for reasoning and questioning.

On the other hand, the more societies become complex, the more difficult for morality to operate as a purely automatic mechanism. Circumstancrs are never the same, and as a result the rules of morality require intelligence in their application. Society is continually evolving; morality itself must be sufficiently flexible to change gradually as proves necessary. But this requires that morality not be internalized in such a way as to be beyond criticism or reflection, the agents par excellence of all change. Individuals, while conforming, must take account of what they are doing; and their conformity must not be pushed to the point where it completely captures intelligence. Thus, it does not follow from a belief in the need for discipline that discipline must involve blind and slavish submission. Moral rules must be invested with that authority without which they would be ineffective. However, since a certain point in history it has not been necessary to remove authority from the realm of discussion, converting it into icons to which man dare not, so to speak, lift his eyes. We shall have to inquire later how it is possible to meet these two, apparently contradictory, requirements. For the moment it must suffice to point them out.

This matter leads us to examine an objection that may already have occurred to you. We have contended that the erratic, the undisciplined, are morally incomplete. Do they not, nevertheless, play a morally useful part in society? Was not Christ such a deviant, as well as Socrates? And is it not thus with all the historical figures whose names we associate with the great moral revolutions through which humanity has passed? Had their feeling of respect for the moral rules characteristic of their day been too lively, they would not have undertaken to alter them. To dare to shake off the yoke of traditional discipline, one should not feel authority too strongly. Nothing could be clearer.

However, if in critical and abnormal circumstances the feeling for the rule and for discipline must be weakened, it does not follow that such impairment is normal. Furthermore, we must take care not to confuse two very different feelings: the need to substitute a new regulation for an old one; and the impatience with all rules, the abbhorrence of all discipline. Under orderly conditions, the former is natural, healthy, and fruitful; the latter is always abnormal since it prompts us to alienate ourselves from the basic conditions of life. Doubtless, with some of the great moral innovators, a legitimate need for change has degenerated into something like anarchy. Because the rules prevailing in their time offended them deeply, their sense of the evil led them to blame, not this or that particular and trainsient form of moral discipline, but the principle itself of all discipline. But it is precisely this that always vitiated their efforts; it is this that rendered so many revolutions fruitless, not yielding results corresponding to the effort expended.

Bibliography of Durkheim's Major Works

ORIGINAL WORKS

(Durkheim's books, including those which appeared posthumously, were first published in Paris by Felix Alcan, unless otherwise stated.)

1983 *De la division du travail social: étude sur l'organisation des sociétés supérieures*.

1895 *Les règles de la méthode sociologique*.

1897 *Le suicide: étude de sociologie*.

1903 (with Marcel Mauss) 'De quelques formes primitives de classification; contribution a l'étude des représentations collectives', *L'Année sociologique*, vol. 6, pp. 1–72.

1912 *Les formes élémentaires de la vie religieuse: le système totémique en Australie*.

Published posthumously

1922 *Education et sociologie*. Introduction by Paul Fauconnet.

1924 *Sociologie et philosophe*. Preface by Celestin Bouglé.

1925 *L'Education morale*. Foreword by P. Fauconnet.

1928 *Le socialisme: sa définition, ses débuts, la doctrine Saint-Simonienne*. Introduction by Marcel Mauss, Paris. Presses Universitaires de France.

1938 *L'Evolution pédagogique en France.* Introduction by Maurice Halbwachs; two volumes.

1950 *Lecons de sociologie: physique des moeurs et du droit.* Foreword by H. Nail Kubali; introduction by Georges Davy, Istanbul: L'université d'Istanbul, and Paris: Presses Universitaires de France.

1955 *Pragmatisme et sociologie.* Reconstructed from students' notes by Armand Cuvillier, Paris: Vrin.

ENGLISH TRANSLATIONS

(Dates are those of hardback editions, whereas references in text include paperback editions.)

1915 *The Elementary Forms of the Religious Life: a Study in Religious Sociology.* Trans. Joseph Ward Swain, London: Allen & Unwin; New York: Macmillan.

1933 *The Division of Labour in Society.* Trans. with an introduction by George Simpson, New York: Macmillan. (New translation by W. D. Halls, London: Macmillan, 1984.)

1938 *The Rules of Sociological Method.* Trans. Sarah A. Solovay and John H. Mueller; introduction by George E. G. Catlin, Chicago: University of Chicago Press. (New translation by W. D. Halls, London: Macmillan, 1982.)

1951 *Suicide: a Study in Sociology.* Trans. John A. Spaulding and George Simpson; introduction by George Simpson, Glencoe: Free Press; London: Routledge & Kegan Paul, 1952.

1953 *Sociology and Philosophy.* Trans. D. F. Pocock; introduction by J. G. Peristiany, London: Cohen & West; Glencoe: Free Press.

1956 *Education and Sociology.* Trans. with an introduction by Sherwood D. Fox; Foreword by Talcot Parsons, Glencoe; Free Press.

1957 *Professional Ethics and Civic Morals.* Translation of *Lecons de Sociologie* by Cornelia Brookfield, London: Routledge & Kegan Paul.

1958 *Socialism and Saint-Simon* (subsequently entitled *Socialism*). Trans. Charlotte Sattler; introduction by Alvin W. Gouldner, Yellow Springs: Antioch Press; London: Routledge & Kegan Paul, 1959.

1960 *Montesquieu and Rousseau.* Trans. Ralph Manheim. Ann Arbor: University of Michigan Press.

1961 *Moral Education: a Study in the Theory and Application of the Sociology of Education.* Trans. Everett K. Wilson and Herman Schnurer; introduction by Everett K. Wilson, Glencoe: Free Press

1963 *Primitive Classification*. Trans. with an introduction by Rodney Needham, London: Cohen & West; Chicago: University of Chicago Press.
1977 *The Evolution of Educational Thought*. Trans. Peter Collins, London: Routledge & Kegan Paul.

ESSAYS AND REVIEWS

Bellah, Robert N. (ed.) *Emile Durkheim on Morality and Society*, Chicago: University of Chicago Press, 1973.

Duvignaud, Jean (ed.) *Journal Sociologique*, Paris: Presses Universitaires de France, 1969.

Nandon, Yash (ed.) *Emile Durkheim; Contributions to L'Année Sociologique*, London: Collier-Macmillan; New York: Free Press, 1980.

Filloux, Jean-Claude (ed.), Emile Durkheim, *La Science Sociale et l'Action*, Paris: Presses Universitaires de France, 1970.

Traugott, Mark (ed.) *Emile Durkheim on Institutional Analysis*, Chicago: University of Chicago Press, 1978.

KEY TEXTS
Series Editor: Peter Hamilton

READINGS FROM EMILE DURKHEIM

Editor: KENNETH THOMPSON
Reader in Sociology, The Open University

Emile Durkheim is regarded as a "founding father" of sociology, and is studied in all basic sociology courses. There is, however, a distinct lack of a handy textbook to provide a satisfactory collection of the key passages from Durkheim's work.

Kenneth Thompson makes good that gap in the literature, providing a collection of modern and reliable translations from the sociologist's major works, *De la division du travail social* (1893), *Les règles de la méthode sociologique* (1895), *Le suicide* (1897) and *Les formes élémentaires de la vie réligieuse* (1912). This text, a useful reference with in-depth coverage, will have a wide appeal to students of sociology at all levels. It complements the author's own commentary in the *Key Sociologists* series (Horwood/Tavistock), *Emile Durkheim* (1982); at the same time, it remains a free-standing work in its own right.

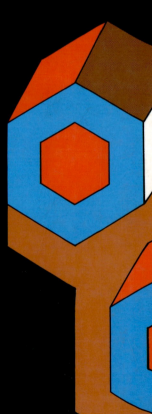

11 New Fetter Lane
London EC4P 4EE

29 West 35th Street
New York NY 10001

ISBN 0-415-04320-4

9 780415 043205